MAR̲̲̲̲̲̲̲̲̲̲̲̲̲ ̲̲̲̲̲̲̲̲̲̲̲̲̲̲̲̲̲̲̲̲̲̲̲̲es-
burg ̲̲̲̲̲̲̲̲̲̲̲̲̲̲̲̲̲̲̲̲̲̲̲̲̲̲̲̲̲̲̲̲ical
pract̲̲̲̲̲̲̲̲̲̲̲̲̲̲̲̲̲̲̲̲̲̲̲̲̲̲̲̲̲̲ to
Brita̲̲̲̲̲̲̲̲̲̲̲̲̲̲̲̲̲̲̲̲̲̲̲̲̲̲on.
In parallel with that he became
increasingly involved in psychological and
spiritual investigation, that culminated in
his ordination to the Anglican priesthood
in 1975.

He lectures on pathology at the Royal
College of Surgeons of England, and is also
priest-in-charge of the church of Holy
Trinity with All Saints in London. He is
constantly engaged in the ministry of
counselling and healing, and in conducting
retreats all over the country.

Dr Israel has written a considerable
number of books including *Summons to
Life, Precarious Living, Smouldering Fire,
The Pain That Heals* (these published by
Mowbrays), *Living Alone* (SPCK), *The
Spirit of Counsel* (Hodder & Stoughton),
Healing as Sacrament (Darton, Longman
& Todd), *The Discipline of Love* (SPCK)
and *Coming in Glory* (Darton, Longman &
Todd).

MARTIN ISRAEL

GETHSEMANE

The Transfiguring Love

With a Foreword by the
Archbishop of Canterbury

Collins
FOUNT PAPERBACKS
in association with Faith Press

I am grateful to Noel Dermot O'Donoghue
for some helpful insights contained in his
writings

First published in 1987 by Fount Paperbacks, London
in association with Faith Press

Copyright © Martin Israel 1987
Made and printed in Great Britain by
William Collins Sons and Co.Ltd, Glasgow

If I go forward, he is not there;
if backward, I cannot find him;
when I turn left, I cannot descry him;
I face right, but I see him not.
But he knows me in action or at rest;
when he tests me, I prove to be gold.

Job 23: 8–10

Who then devised this torment? Love.
Love is the unfamiliar Name
Behind the hands that wove
The intolerable shirt of flame
Which human power cannot remove.
   We only live, only suspire
   Consumed by either fire or fire.

From *Little Gidding* by T.S.Eliot

Contents

Foreword

In *Gethsemane – The Transfiguring Love*, Martin Israel shares his wealth of understanding and wisdom. There is penetrating and sensible psychology. There is profound knowledge of the Bible, sensitively applied. There is a powerful style of exposition, the more authoritative for its simplicity.

All these elements combine to offer the outline of a theology of redemption which is rooted in our understanding of pain. In the dark night of Gethsemane, we learn to accept suffering, not to reject or resent it. Innocent pain can lead us closer to spiritual maturity.

An important insight here – and there are many – is that the Church at its best is a community of sufferers. The Church is most at home with its true vocation when it kneels with Jesus in Gethsemane. That's never easy, either to perceive or to practise. But, as Dr Israel makes plain, it is fundamental to Christian faith that only the way of the Cross can lead to the perfect peace of God.

Robert Canhian

September 1986

Prologue

The chill impact of hell's darkness fell on Jesus at Gethsemane. His agony was especially terrible because it was essentially incommunicable. It is a wonderful thing to be able to share our inmost thoughts with those we love, but there was no one to hear him in his agony. In his great encounter with the naked power of evil Jesus had no one to sustain him, for even his Father seemed to be shut out from his sight by the acrid fumes of impenetrable darkness that enveloped him. And yet, unaided by any outside power, the Son achieved a victory over darkness and suffering due entirely to the power of the Holy Spirit within him.

When Abraham was put to the ultimate test of faith in preparing to sacrifice to God his beloved son Isaac, a ram caught by its horns in a thicket appeared in time to avert Isaac's death. But there was no substitute for Jesus; he went to his death in unrelieved suffering. Yet by that very suffering he removed the despair that comes with it, as in his death he removed the apparent finality of death and the consequent vanity of so much mortal life. In his great work in the realms of darkness, the divine presence moved decisively from a point of remote sovereignty outside the cosmos to the centre of the created world, to the centre of the human soul. And so the Godhead, far beyond rational thought and intellectual speculation, is now firmly centred in the soul of all who have faith, who have thereby passed from the barrier of death to the measureless expanse of eternal life. The test of that faith remains, but victory is now assured to all who persist to the end. The reward is the emergence of a new person, strangely like the one originally born, but now cleansed of the world's stain, chaste in purpose and innocent in intent and attitude.

It is this theme that we consider in what follows: how we too can partake of the divine nature by entering into the depth of Christ's passion, not merely in the course of a Lenten meditation but by the progress of our chequered lives on earth. The way of ascent to the vision of God embraces a precarious treading of the precipice that leads to hell. Only when hell is restored can we bear the intensity of God's love.

1

From the Unreal to the Real

In a cold temperate climate the blazing sun is a friendly presence. As its rays impinge on us, so the body expands in joyful response, and even the taut emotional life relaxes for a moment. We may even smile in unconscious thanksgiving and see some pleasant prospect ahead of us. Then its beneficent rays are unobtrusively intercepted by clouds; its presence seems to recede, and a chill enfolds us, both in body and mind. It brings to our inner awareness the transience of all things beautiful and comforting, the realization of how short-lived our periods of happiness are, invariably succeeded by episodes of frustration as our plans are interrupted and our hopes delayed.

In due course the sun ends its daily circuit and sets in the west; darkness falls, covering our portion of the globe. This we take in our stride, for we know that the sun's influence is never at an end even when it is invisible; without it our lives would perish in an instant. We fall sound asleep during the dark pall of the night with the beautiful trust of a little child – who is indeed our true stature irrespective of the distinction we may have attained in the world. We are confident that we will awaken to the light of another day, fresh for new experiences to fulfil our destiny, of whose nature we are both ignorant and yet dimly aware at the same time. And in the day we do our work, encouraged by the sun's radiance and subdued into pensive reflection by the dullness induced by a cloudy sky. Darkness and light succeed each other day by day, yet we respond to Jesus' observation, "While daylight lasts we must carry on the work of him who sent me; night comes, when no one can work" (John 9:4). He goes on to say that while he is in the world he is the light of the world. But what is the nature of the darkness of the night that we are due to experience, first physically but later spiritually also? We confront the earthly darkness with a faith in the workings of the natural order, but what is the basis of the faith that may guide us through the darkness of the inner man? This is the soul, the organ of intimate identity where we may make judgements of value and then commit ourselves to abide by them. The action of the soul in doing this work is the free will.

This deeper darkness confronts us in our private lives, our hidden solitude, from the time that we are aware of our separate unique identity, of which our special name is an outer mark of meaning that distinguishes us from all other people. The youth may confront the challenges of life with apparent indifference as he surmounts them without difficulty, but his sensitive soul flinches at the shafts of criticism and misunderstanding that are an inevitable burden of daily life; they cast a foreboding shadow on the horizon but are easily dismissed as he continues on his breathless way. As life progresses the heavier clouds of competition, jealousy and failure cast a darker, more persistent shadow which becomes doubly threatening as the corruption of the world adds to its power. A person is coming to age psychologically, in mind and soul, when he learns to accept that no human agency is likely to advance his career, that his future prosperity depends on himself alone using the gifts with which he has been endowed. When human support fails, or at least reaches its limit, he may make the sudden discovery of a deeper source of help, one that is constant and always available. Its presence lies within him, the awareness of God, who is in fact both an external source of love and a deeper indwelling within the soul. But how few of us attain that degree of spiritual knowledge, which shows itself outwardly as an emotional maturity that gives of itself and does not look for rewards and praise! The happy few who have made the transition from human dependence to divine service have scaled one level of darkness, and can face the flux of day and night with a degree of composure that is independent of material circumstances, being anchored in a sea of spiritual values.

Most of us, however, look with distaste on the advent of ageing. We dread the encroachment of each year into the glow of our present security, for it brings with it a chill that presages increasing impotence in life's struggle, loneliness and physical enfeeblement. The moment of truth about the basic human condition generally, and our own more particularly, has a darkness about it that is so forbidding that its advent is delayed for as long as possible by a fevered participation in the affairs of the present moment. This participation is one of escape rather than direct awareness, and therefore its role is to shield us from reality rather than to bring us closer to our true end. The darkness may be banished by the artificial light of worldly diversions, but in due course that light flickers and is then extinguished. How dark then is the ensuing gloom!

The gloom is intensified as the flow of relationships,

on which the life of the person depends, is menaced by the inroads of the death of those close to us. We accept their support without acknowledgement in the course of the day; we almost forget their contribution to the memorable experiences of our life, little realizing that it is their presence which is the essence of most of the beauty in our existence. As the sun descends and declines in the west, so do our lives fade away on a mute note of sadness: too late have we discovered what was crucially important for us in eternity, too little have we done to ennoble the world and heal its creatures. But deep within us there flickers a spark of hope, a belief that a new day will dawn with more experiences to be tasted, more wisdom to be acquired, more love to be shown. The spark burns from the spirit deeply placed in the soul, the point of contact between God and us. This is the seat of the highest judgements of value. We read in Numbers 3:38 that in the course of the exodus of the Israelites from Egyptian slavery and the arrival in the Promised Land, Moses was stationed with Aaron and his sons in front of the Tabernacle on the east. They were stationed in front of the Tent of Presence towards the sunrise. This is a beautiful symbol of the inextinguishable nature of human aspiration towards mortal completion and the vision of God. As the Israelites followed the way of the sunrise to reach their glorious destination, so also do we advance by hope, strengthened by faith, towards our destined end, which is God.

The way, alas, is neither uniformly well lit nor is it of even contour. It is interrupted by dark, precipitous valleys of such magnitude that we can all too easily lose our way, indeed our very bearings, in them. Then it seems as if we have taken the wrong path, made the wrong journey, and that we are to be swallowed up, like travellers lost in a vast desert, in oblivion. But we have to go on, for there is no obvious place of turning back, any more than the ungrateful, intransigent Israelites could really return to Egypt, with all its enticements recalled to mind but none of the harsh punishment of the slavedrivers. One cannot turn back; indeed, no one who sets his hand to the plough and then keeps looking back is fit for the kingdom of God (Luke 9:62). Turning back, or even gazing nostalgically towards the past, is tantamount to committing suicide, to cursing God, to turning one's face to the wall and dying. The living darkness at least teaches us something about eternity: in it we learn that we are nothing in our own right, that all identity based on the world's power is an illusion, that our very concepts of reality, determined by worldly models, are vain. We learn that the ultimate reality to which we grope has no relation to anything we may conceive mentally, but is to be understood intuitively as the supreme No-Thing, in the same way that we are also nothing apart from it. And yet from this ineffable No-Thing flows the love and power that creates and sustains all things, even ourselves. The knowledge that emerges out of this debris of shattered illusion is our true inheritance; a love that shows itself in absolute dereliction is our reward. We begin to understand the teaching of St Paul, in 1 Corinthians 13:2, that faith in God sufficient to move mountains, but without love, is vain. Indeed, that faith may have to be all but shattered before we can begin to know love. The darkness is here to teach us about love in utter hopelessness; then alone may we be filled with the No-Thing that leaves us complete.

It must also be said that the way is, in addition, interspersed with high mountains which it is our privilege to scale, aided by the grace of God. At their peak we see the Promised Land as did the dying Moses: "Then Moses went up from the lowlands of Moab to Mount Nebo, to the top of Pisgah, eastwards from Jericho, and the Lord showed him the whole land" (Deuteronomy 34:1). He was allowed to see it all with his own eyes, but he could not cross over into it, because he had proved himself unworthy of that supreme privilege. Likewise, the great mystics have seen the heavenly realm from the peak of the mountain of illumination where the uncreated light of God is the ground of eternity. But then they have had to descend to the lower depths once more, as did Peter, James and John after their vision of the Lord Jesus in his transcendent glory on the Mount of Transfiguration. And Jesus himself had to descend fearfully yet triumphantly to the darkest of all valleys.

In an alley sloping downwards and imperceptibly darkening as its contours are assayed, we can see a number of people who are, in fact, representatives of the human condition. Previously they had all led successful lives, at least by worldly standards, their very prosperity separating them from the general run of their fellows in a self-contained style of living, complacent, assured and insensitive. And then the bastion of their security was summarily removed – in real life that removal is usually sudden and precipitate, for until then they had lived in selfish unawareness both of themselves and of the world around them. The collapse is total; the light of assurance is extinguished, and all that is left is a void containing a distracted individual groping vainly for a landmark of orientation, a trace of identification. There seems to be no one to help as the world pursues its heedless course. It is a sad fact that most of us are as oblivious of our communal responsibility to a wounded fellow as the priest and Levite in the Parable of the Good Samaritan. To be fair to human nature, it responds with alacrity to anyone who is physically hurt, but it is less helpful to those whose wound is deeper and therefore less obvious. It is noteworthy, furthermore, that in the parable the one who comes to the assistance of the victim of robbery with violence is a Samaritan, a heretic outside the pale of the local community. It may well be that his bitter experience of ostracism, rejection and loneliness made him especially conscious of the traveller's plight and sensitive to his isolation. In this moment of recognition the outsider could identify himself with the victim. This is indeed a small fruit of suffering patiently endured or an injustice borne without recrimination. Society at large, by contrast, is often blind and cruel, because like the crowd who witnessed Jesus' crucifixion, it does not know what it is doing. It must be admitted that the indifference of the mass of humanity is seldom appreciably altered by the virtue of a person it has rejected, for most of us are so immersed in our own private fantasies that we are seldom available to see anything outside ourselves. In fact, the potential will to good among most people is considerable, but before this can be activated a considerable shock is often necessary to break into the general apathy. It is this blind indifference with its total unawareness that can be so terrifying in a mass of people; a few may be moved by the disinterested concern and transparent holiness of an individual member, but most remain untouched. In the darkness the deeper challenges of life may, paradoxically, be far better seen and confronted, so that a definite decision can be made: whether we are to declare ourselves for or against a commitment to become authentic people, manifest children of God.

And so those about to enter the valley of darkness disappear from the general view. They see themselves accurately for the first time in their lives as little children exposed to the inclement elements of existence, against which they had been so tightly insulated by the security they had achieved. There is the general atmosphere of bereavement, the stripping away of a relationship or a circumstance around which the life of the person had previously revolved. Bereavement in this general formulation includes much more than the death of a loved one, with which the term is usually associated. A person may be dispossessed of his employment which was the bastion of his sense of self-esteem, to say nothing of the financial consequences of the calamity. Usually it is an immaterial thing that has been taken away: a betrayal of one's trust, a repudiation of the love one had borne a marriage partner in the sordid business of infidelity, a throwing up in one's face of one's inner social insecurity based on racial or religious grounds. Previously an edifice of security, even propriety, had been erected to conceal the unsure foundations of one's origin, and now the whole contrivance is demolished. One stands once more as a little child, cowering at the world's disdain. In fact most of the disdain is a creation of one's own unsteady mind; the world goes on oblivious of one's hurt. It is the past with its insecurity and fear that dominates the consciousness of the victim, and this he projects onto the present situation. An insult of the long past, if it remains dormant and its emotional charge is not spent, comes back forcibly into one's mind, and brings one back to one's situation at that time. Perhaps one was a mere child then, but the memory allied to the present bereavement can easily cut one down to the size of a child, flinching from yet railing against the injustice of life. The darkness becomes more intense as hope is excluded and one is surrounded by the dank coldness of isolation: nobody cares and one is left behind to perish in oblivion.

The general run of society has little use for failures, whether these be enterprises that falter or people who do not make the grade according to the world's criteria of success or respectability. The same condemnation holds true, unfortunately, in many instances of religious renewal. Its protagonists are all too often perplexed by those among them who fail to show a radical transformation of character or a conspicuous inner healing of some embarrassing impediment. To them success proves that God is with them; indeed success can easily become a very proof of God's power, even his existence. In this way their pattern of belief and its ensuing course of action is proved to be divinely inspired. But when one of their members fails to reach the mark or attain an outer, manifest healing, they tend to cast the burden of his condition squarely in his face: perhaps his faith was insufficient or else unacknowledged sin was lurking in the background. That God's ways of healing may be beyond mortal comprehension is often a proposition that lies outside their simplistic, emotional range of understanding; admittedly Jesus healed the sick, but he was unable to save himself from a particularly ignominious death on the cross between two criminals. From their point of view it is better that the unhealed member should be discharged forthwith from the company of the elect, so that their easy assurance may not be too severely challenged. The failed person can thus conveniently be expelled from their midst and be submerged in the amorphous hell of secular society, left to drown in a mass of faceless people. These jostle each other while pushing and straining to attain an end which is an illusion.

And so it comes about that the summary dismissal of an apparently doomed person may be the initial movement forced upon him towards his attainment of the light, a light illuminating a trackless waste whose contours remain uncharted. But at least it has a strange authenticity which is lacking in so much of the formal social scene. In this scene his associates want to have as little to do with him as possible because involvement is menacing. It brings one too close to the brink of one's own insecurity, to the moment of truth which one would delay as long as possible. Once one concerns oneself with another person's plight, one exposes oneself to his psychic emanations, to the sharpness of his pain. At the same time one tends to distance oneself from the company of the prosperous and successful, with whom, in one's baser moments, one would like to be identified. By contrast, the ones who have been stripped of all with which they have previously identified themselves are attaining an authenticity that they previously lacked. Indeed, they are coming together in the darkness, and a fellowship, as yet intangible, is forming even though the participants are scarcely aware of each other. This type of unforced fellowship is common to all those who lie incarcerated, whether in gaols for criminal offenders or in prison camps set aside for political or religious deviants. Their antecedents may be questionable, but their future has a common destiny. They may either perish on a note of despair or else go on into a new life of purification. The good and the bad share a common abode. In the way ahead a new identity is to be forged for each one of them.

2

The Path of Suffering: The Descent

The path of suffering ahead of those who have been bereaved of that which made their lives meaningful, which assured a precious existence to be protected against the assaults of injury and accident, is one of inner emptiness and outer loneliness. Of the two it is the inner experience that is the more terrifying. It is above all the descent into a void, a chasm that chills the soul and fills the mind with terror. The void is soon filled with material from the unconscious that had previously been censored and kept at bay. All that was secretly feared in the past, that was inflicted on one in one's early years and kept repressed in the depths of silence, is now released. And so one begins to live in a world of primitive terror, of subterranean unease. Nothing can be withheld from the void that was previously occupied by the person or circumstance now departed.

The memory is exquisitely sensitive, so that any object or event that even remotely stirs up the mind produces an unbearable tension. In the end it is a nameless dread that envelops one as one realizes that the past is beyond healing and the future is problematic. The present, always a point of contact with the eternal as it transcends duration, is a chasm of impenetrable gloom. The psychic debris of past times and indeed generations assaults the one groping his way in the gloom. It speaks of fear, torture and extinction, and it emits a pungent odour of panic and horror that can all but annihilate the personality. And there is no help from outside, apart from drugs that might dull the emotional pain, inducing a state of sleep. In this respect it is noteworthy that the body often responds to unhappiness and discouragement by fatigue and somnolence: the oblivion, though temporary, serves the dual function of softening the distress and marshalling the inner resources of hope and faith which may see the sufferer through the immediate state of hell.

For the person who is awake and alert, the suffering of rejection can be especially cruel, but in that darkness he may become aware of another soul in similar pain. To be sure, the awareness is primarily psychic – from soul to soul directly without recourse to verbal or intellectual communication. When it becomes obvious that the past cannot be retrieved and that the way forward is inevitable, a strength is given one that comes from a source outside the personality, although intimately involved in it. The strength comes not only from the divine presence, but also from other people who are in distress or who, even more significantly, have traversed the valley of desolation and are now available to guide and encourage their compatriots struggling through the morass of fear, ignorance and hopelessness. As Pascal said, we would not seek God had we not found him; this encounter is in the depth of the soul which has now been opened to us as the void widens to disclose insights beyond our normal selfish preoccupation. To proceed to traverse the valley of the shadow of death in faith, groping blindly in the thick fog of spiritual darkness, is to know God in a very different way from that proclaimed in traditional religion or conventional piety. This new manifestation of the divine fills the soul with hope, not so much of personal salvation as of communal deliverance. Once we can get beyond our own hurts and grievances, we can begin to know our fellows in the darkness and assume their burden of grief also. In so doing there is an exchange of suffering, and the burden becomes measurably lighter.

Indeed, a new fellowship has been initiated and forged in the flame of suffering. We can begin to talk in a new language, one without guile or subterfuge. It is a language that emanates from the heart, and even when it is unspoken, it is fully intelligible to all those in the valley of desolation. At first the sufferer is encompassed in his own misfortune, and his mind ranges in futile, though masochistic, circles of resentment and imagined revenge. In so doing, he maintains a contact with his past life and can even, in his imagination, put himself into a realm of reinstatement and power. If the tragedy has been the death of a loved one, there is less resentment to be aired, at least against earthly powers, but a deeper hatred of the whole creative process has to be acknowledged, and this centres ultimately on the conventional figure of God. This is the same type of God against whom Job contested so vehemently; it is in fact the God of the theologians, who is so often a mental construct rather than a living reality. The God of the philosophers is indeed of a different calibre to the God of Abraham, Isaac and Jacob, whom Pascal was privileged to see in his famous illumination. All who suffer are to see that God as well if, like Job, they have the courage to persist in the journey through the darkness. This persistence is not simply pious self-denigration; it is also self-affirmation in the image of one's true being.

In the darkness we can be ourselves and cease to live the lie of successful people. What comes up to us can be accepted without flinching from it or trying to mollify it by psychological or sociological expertise. It is ourselves, and also an aspect of the unconscious life common to all mankind, if not all rational creatures. When we realize this, a great barrier between ourselves and others begins to lift, so that we may start to glimpse a new type of community emerging from the debris of past preconceptions and illusions. It must, however, in stark realism be said that this community does not take root spontaneously, nor is its establishment rapid. Even in our pain, with fierce tenacity we tend to cling onto past roots, since these appear to establish our identity. At the same time, we can blame other people, ranged into social, racial or religious classes, for our own suffering. A scapegoat is an especially satisfactory target onto which to project, even to jettison, our unhappiness. Then we can relieve ourselves in a cesspit of hatred, while overlooking the real cause of our suffering – the selfish life of the past and our membership in the community of people whose suffering we must accept no less than the security it affords.

Ezekiel diagnosed the human condition well when he spoke about hearts of stone. He also saw correctly the divine power of healing in terms of awakening those frigid hearts to the vibrancy of life, the life of the flesh. If we all had hearts that beat in unison with the music of creation, that palpitated in the face of cruelty and rose up in sympathy to support even one creature in distress, the world would be transfigured.

The darkness of those in the depths of suffering is in fact continuous with the darkness of the visible world where we all lead our self-centred existences, even when we pay lip service to the ideals of true religion and piety. But whereas the victim is freed to confront that darkness as part of his journey towards the light, the majority of those living comfortably in the world have not even begun to glimpse both its darkness and the supernatural light on which all creation depends for its sustenance and its eventual transformation. When those imprisoned in the darkness of suffering can begin to glimpse this light of God whose uncreated energies sustain the universe, they will have made their great movement to a new world where pain is lifted up in triumph. But the way is outside human contrivance.

As the pain continues, so the traveller senses others on the path, not only the bereaved who lament the passing into extinction of the joy they once knew, but also those whose deprival is of a more urgent quality. These are the physically and mentally handicapped, and the millions who are destined to spend their whole lives in squalor. Some are in this extreme destitution because of their own inadequacy, but many more are the victims of social injustice and human improvidence. The wretched of the earth inhabit large areas of the undeveloped countries where a small social élite lives in luxury while the bulk of their fellows stagnate in a poverty that knows no ending. In this degradation the human character rots until it becomes a purely animal consciousness. It must be said also, however, that poverty in itself does not necessarily degrade a person, any more than affluence exalts him. It is the human solidarity in our situation that binds together the units into a composite whole. The social realist may deride the spirituality of communal poverty and the religious tradition on which that spirituality hangs. If this opium could only be removed, the people would wake up and take their plight into their own hands. While there is some truth in this condemnation of religion – pageantry often thrives on the poverty and exploitation of the masses – the matter is more intricate than this. Spirituality is a natural quality of the soul, as necesssary for its workings as are air and food for the health of the body; its incarnation into a living religious tradition is a very necessary part of the life of a community. In those countries where traditional religion is banned, an ideology has, at least to some extent, subtly replaced the previous spiritual expression of the people. The results are seldom impressive, either in terms of the general well-being or even the overall economic situation. The root of the human problem is meaninglessness rather than poverty, terrible as this may be in terms of human dignity. If life did have meaning that transcended the mere stimulation of the senses and led people on to an encounter with the eternal truths, war would give way to peace, and poverty would be dealt with creatively by a much more just distribution of resources. At the moment, this aspiration seems purely visionary, but until it becomes a practical issue there will be no end of suffering. Those who are going through the pit of darkness are glimpsing this truth, for at least the old values that sustained them are being revealed in their naked inadequacy.

The great impediment to all human progress is the dominance of the ego-consciousness. However, the ego, which may be seen as the expression of the person's identity in the world of forms and matter, is not in itself bad – indeed, without it the person could not do the particular work that he had been called upon to perform during his mortal life. In this respect it is as necessary as the physical body. But when either the ego or the body claims a dominant position in the personality, it takes over the person and starts to war with anyone who threatens its power and thwarts its ambitions. It demands recompense, and is offended when it fails to get its due recognition. The Parable of the Labourers in the Vineyard (Matthew 20:1–16) portrays the pretensions of the ego very clearly: each labourer seeks his own, and is extremely annoyed when someone else gets the same reward as he. He should have been attending to his own condition instead of prying into that of the other person; he should have been grateful for the payment of his own previously agreed wages, rather than comparing these with those of the workers who joined him later in the day. In the world of material values and workaday commerce the complaints of the early workers are justified; in the world of eternal values they are merely puerile, for we are all members one of another, parts of the same body, and the very concept of an atomistic ego is absurd. What is for my good, in the larger life, is for the common good also. Conversely, in the words of John Donne, "Any man's death diminishes me, because I am involved in mankind". All these considerations, so alien to the world of affairs that we inhabit in our time of prosperity, become clearer to the person in pain that cannot be relieved, in suffering that refuses to be ameliorated.

As the descent into darkness proceeds, so the claims

of the ego become muted, as if by sheer exhaustion. It is wrong to submit to life's misfortunes, to the apparent slings and arrows of a dark, inscrutable fate, with a bovine passivity. It is far more productive spiritually to accept them actively, and this acceptance usually follows a period of furious revolt; Job himself disputed angrily through the medium of his comforters with the unseen God, an attitude of sharp questioning apparent also in a number of the Psalms. It is to the credit of the disputant that he takes his suffering seriously enough to bewail it and cast doubts about the ultimate love of God, or else the power of God to control the universe he had created. Now at least the realm of theology is being broached even if the victim affirms a negatively atheistic point of view. In the end the mind does look for a first cause of creation which the soul clothes with a personality that can be questioned and arraigned. This is probably as near the existence of God as the rational mind can attain: he is already known in the depths of the soul, but before he can be of positive help to us he must be made intellectually available. As Isaiah puts it, "Surely God is among you and there is no other, no other god. How then canst thou be a god that hideth thyself, O God of Israel, the deliverer?" (Isaiah 45:14f). In fact, he is hidden from us until we make ourselves available to receive him. In a state of suffering the dross of worldly glamour is taken from us, and we are more open to the divine presence. But first the ego has to become a servant of the soul, and we have to proceed with the ignorance of little children. The process is a long, arduous one. I believe in fact that the ego cannot be set aside in its claims of justice and reward until it is changed by divine grace.

Until then the creature continues to grope in the darkness of suffering which he makes his own hell, cursing life, fate, God, or whatever concept he has of ultimate reality. But, in fact, he is as far from God as the religious fanatics who, through the ages, have destroyed those disagreeing with them. The purely human understanding has first to come to terms with the divine reality of love before the transformation can occur.

As the darkness gathers, so does the terror increase. The person made redundant faces a hell of inanimacy. Even if his economic state is viable, so that he is in no danger of poverty, he is out in the cold of the world's respect. He is like the solitary figure on a frozen railway platform, with the trains rushing by but none stopping to receive him. A terrible emptiness encompasses him as he sees into a future of meaningless inactivity. It is like death with no one to care about his situation. The person bereaved of a loved one is likewise out in the cold. There is no one to share the intimate experiences of life as they flow by, day after day. The capacity to share and enjoy life's pageant with another person is fundamental to the well-being of us all. All real living is meeting, says Martin Buber in his book *I and Thou*. Once the supreme Thou in our life has departed from us, we are left with a collection of "Its", with whom we can engage in conversation but among whom we cannot communicate from the depth of the soul. It is this deeper psychic communion that is the basis of a true meeting. When all was going well with us, we could prosper quite plausibly on a number of "I-It" relationships that occupied our time pleasurably but inconsequentially. Now all this has been taken from us, and our inner spiritual bankruptcy is made apparent. This is the basis of a terrible void, one in which we are cut off from the awareness of all those around us except for the rare person who has been to hell himself and has experienced resurrection. But will we ever be able to follow the course of regeneration known to that enviable person?

We can at this juncture visualize the course of the Prodigal Son in Jesus' most famous parable. When he leaves the protection of his father's house and ventures forth into the wider world, he thinks only of himself, his sensual desires dominating his field of awareness. He uses every person he encounters as a tool for his lust and gluttony, so that his relationships are of the I-It type. Then he loses his inheritance and falls into penury. While he tends the pigs who seem to have more than he, a voice speaks with authority from deep within himself: it is the Spirit of God speaking from his own spirit. In the darkness of a hell he has inflicted upon himself because of his selfish improvidence, he has lost the company of all those who were his friends during his time of profligacy. When he descended into darkness, they vanished out of sight, and there is none left to support him. In his dereliction he has attained a quiet attentiveness sufficient to hear the still, small voice of God speaking within him, a voice that moves him to truth and humility. It shows him a way of approach to reality: an honest appraisal of the past, conscious acknowledgement which ends in a confession, and a commitment to amend his future way of life. He returns in sincere repentance and can, for the first time in his life, effect an I-Thou relationship with his father, whose joyful relief at receiving his son intact overrides any possible anger he might have felt for the son's irresponsible behaviour.

It is the recognition of God that has effected the conversion of the young man from profligacy to honest labour. But would that recognition have taken place without the period of intense humiliation and pain, without the experience of traversing the valley of the shadow of death? In the case of most of us the answer is probably in the negative, because we tend to lead lives of blind self-gratification until the blow strikes. In the valley of dereliction God's presence – as powerful in hell as in heaven, as Psalm 139 so memorably states – is more immediately felt, since there is less to distract our attention. It is acknowledged, and the hell is passed over and a life of spiritual renewal started. In the parable, if the younger son had not taken the plunge into the wider world with such apparently disastrous results, he would have stayed dutifully at home and probably remained as emotionally stultified, as immature in love, as his angry elder brother. The brother's complaint, his righteous indignation that the returned scapegrace should be so generously received by his father is, of course, fully in accordance with the standards of conventional morality. But both the father and the returned son have moved beyond those standards in the hell each has known: the father mourning for his lost son (like Jacob mourning for Joseph, whom he believed was killed), and the son surrendering his soul to the inclement elements of the world and entering the darkness of despair. Once one has emerged from such hells as these, one's priorities are radically reviewed and one's perspectives are immeasurably broadened.

But how can the understanding of the elder son be broadened? If we were to extend the parable to the time after the festivities had ended and the repentant son had started work in earnest in his father's estate, he would still have had to face his elder brother's hostility. This cannot be dispelled simply by his father's joy; the injustice of it all rankles, and the virtuous son will continue to recall his brother's folly, perhaps indefinitely. The work of penance in store for the reformed sinner would be to reconcile his brother, and this might be quite impossible. How hard it is to break through the shell of an implacably proud person! He is, in fact, in his own hell, though he does not realize it. This, in a way, is the predicament of a loving God in relation to a sinner who refuses to repent and inhabits the region of hell indefinitely. The free will given by God to his rational creatures ensures the capacity of those creatures to spurn God's advances as easily as respond to them. The impasse, whether in respect of the two brothers in the parable or of God and intransigent man in real life, may finally be resolved by such suffering that the proud, unyielding one has to invoke aid, whether fraternal or divine as the case may be, to relieve his distress. In the instance of the two brothers this would mean that, although the elder may continue to nurse in his heart resentment that his sibling has come off so lightly, a time might come in which he was faced with some danger and his brother came at once to his aid, rather like the Good Samaritan in Jesus's other immortal parable. This act of spontaneous mercy would surely break the carapace of the embittered one, and be the basis of a new relationship between them. It should also be said that God is to be found wherever love is shown, but until we are stripped of all illusions and in the darkness of hell, we may remain impervious to the love around us. The human tragedy is not so much one of evil intention as of unawareness.

In the great cosmic battle another Father and Son, in the eternal bringing forth of life out of chaos, are to mourn at the insensitivity of that life to the gift of love. But in that conflict the nature of God will become clearer to mankind as it goes along the path of unknowing, where everything tangible or intangible appears to be an illusion.

3

The Path of Suffering: The Plateau

On some occasions suffering is of comparatively brief duration, being limited to the time in which relief comes, a relief due to the tangible awareness of God's providence. In the Parable of the Prodigal Son as soon as the young man faces the reality of the situation, he becomes open to the voice of God and knows how to proceed. But what if there were no rich father to receive him, and no home to which he could return? How then would he have fared? Much pain goes on indefinitely, and then the sufferer has to cope with it as best he can. He may, of course, at any time renounce life and opt for death and a peaceful oblivion. Suicide in these circumstances has an obvious attraction, but for those with a more profound view of life this solution is seen to be not merely unsatisfactory but also an illusory escape from fundamental problems. They can see that life continues after death of the body, and the person who has deliberately renounced his mortal existence may find himself in a limbo of isolation: his basic problems of character are not only unhealed but there is also attached to him an awareness of sin, a feeling of guilt, not unlike the remorse felt by the Ancient Mariner in Coleridge's poem after his destruction of the beneficent albatross. It should be said that all situations must be judged by the circumstances precipitating them, and the wilful destruction of one's life in a paroxysm of intolerable pain is less blameworthy than if one were to commit suicide to escape the consequences of criminal action now brought to public light. Nevertheless, I am sure it is wiser as well as nobler to endure suffering, as Job did, than to opt out on a note of angry rejection by cursing God and dying.

Once the impossibility of immediate relief or even amelioration of the pain is faced, a new life opens up. One is brought to confront the very basis of reality, the nature of God. At the same time the supports of one's previous existence seem not so much to be disrupted as to dissolve in the general atmosphere. In the gloom an unearthly radiance illuminates not so much the surroundings as one's own being. The soul is laid bare as one becomes like a helpless child in the grip of circumstances beyond one's experience. If the person remains recalcitrant, fearful or immovable he stays on his own, and the darkness of hell surrounds him in his misery. But if one is open to new possibilities and has retained the ability and capacity to remember others in pain, the darkness begins to show a communal aspect: one is no longer alone but is united in suffering with the entire human race, indeed the very cosmos, since the world was created. And in that community of souls apparently lost to the bright world of glittering opportunity there burns a deeper light visible only to the super-sensual faculty that draws the person onwards into an enlarged community. At first he cannot bear this deeper glow, but as he accommodates to it, so he enters a peace previously unknown to him.

It is recorded, in the birth narrative of Jesus according to St Matthew's account, that after the three magi had returned to their own country by another route so as to avoid informing King Herod about the location of the holy child, Herod in his fury had all the children in the vicinity of Bethlehem killed, hoping that Jesus might be among the slain. The Holy Innocents are a prototype of blameless humanity that suffers as a victim of the evil in the world. Somehow their unmerited pain brings light to a dark universe. Those who suffer justly for past misdemeanours tend to rage against the pain, only gradually becoming aware of their part in the process, that their selfish, thoughtless way of life has reaped a just harvest of retribution. Why did it have to happen to me? This is the age-old question of those who suffer as a retribution for a self-centred approach to reality. By contrast, the innocent sufferer goes to his place of testing, the world's testing as much as his own, mute and uncomplaining. We remember the words of Isaiah in respect of the Suffering Servant, "On himself he bore our sufferings, our torments he endured, while we counted him smitten by God, struck down by disease and misery; but he was pierced for our transgressions, tortured for our iniquities; the chastisement he bore is health for us and by his scourging we are healed" (Isaiah 53:4–5). The retributive suffering of the thoughtless masses is purified and sanctified by the redemptive suffering of the innocent. These do not ask why it had to happen to them: somehow they know that they are meant to be surrounded by darkness in a vortex of mystery. They know that the way is steadily forward in the darkness, and that their present demeanour is all that matters in a waste whose sinuous track threatens to peter out at any moment. And what is the track that they follow? It is the light of God in the soul, and the impetus to follow along is the Holy Spirit within them.

This light is often very constant and the warmth surrounding it very comforting for those who suffer for the sake of righteousness. Indeed, in the final Beatitude Jesus teaches that those who have suffered persecution for the cause of right have the kingdom of heaven as a present reality (Matthew 5:10). This kingdom of heaven is not a radiant presence in the world beyond death, as portrayed so often in popular religious art. It is a state of complete psychic openness in which the brotherhood of man is experienced as a cogent reality and the fatherly presence of God is known as an atmosphere of pure love, disinterested, all-embracing and transfiguring in effect. All this, it should be said, is taking place in the realm of deepest human relationships while all are in utmost darkness. The physical pain and the emotional bereavement are not removed so much as assuaged in the radiance of a love that knows no limitation. In any group of victims of injustice and persecution there will be only a few who will have ascended the mount of transfiguration as exquisitely as this. The majority will labour at the foothills, bemoaning their lot, trying to escape or else giving up in total despair. But the leaven of holiness is so all-pervading that even a single saint can perform the work of deliverance defined in Isaiah 61: bringing good news to the humble, binding up the broken-hearted, proclaiming liberty to the captives and release to those in prison.

All this sounds ridiculous inasmuch as saint and sinner alike are all incarcerated in the same hell. But the saint has transcended the physical, and even the psychical, hell and is one with God in eternity. By this divine relationship he is able to lift up the others from their hell of anguish, resentment and isolation to a realm of reconciliation where they can find themselves in a larger company, in a more inclusive framework of relationships, both with each other and with God. Indeed, this may be their first experience of deity.

The plateau of suffering is almost intolerable when we feel alone on it; it becomes increasingly bearable when we can share its landscape with others in their special predicament. Those who live in abject poverty, a circumstance common enough in the undeveloped parts of the world, often have an awareness of spiritual things that seems to be hidden from their more affluent fellows in the developed countries. This awareness is no mere opium to dull their depleted senses and starved bodies; on the contrary, it is an awareness of the eternal dimension that far transcends their mortal plight. The circumstance that facilitates their spiritual awareness is communal solidarity. What is experienced together becomes less frightening, more bearable. In the same way the victims of totalitarian brutality in our own century have, on occasions, risen to a height of spiritual awareness in which they could actively thank God for their torture, not as a gesture of masochistic satisfaction, but as an acknowledgement of the deeper insights into reality that their terrible experience had afforded. The essential insight is that the spiritual is alone fully real, and all else is real only in so far as it sheds light on eternal things. The observation of the early Quaker Isaac Penington is especially relevant: "Every truth is shadow except the last. Yet every truth is substance in its own place, though it be but shadow in another place. And the shadow is true shadow, as the substance is true substance." In other words, all life is sacramental if we dedicate ourselves to God's service and to that of our fellow creatures (indeed, the one is incomplete without the other). If we were fully awake to reality, every action of our life would be noble, and self-preservation would find its completion in service to all life. Then the command to love our neighbour as ourselves would find its fulfilment. This fulfilment, far from renouncing the individual self, sees that self glorified in the midst of a transfigured community. And this is what the community of tortured victims in a prison camp may become, in a way that would be hardly conceivable in a stable group of prosperous citizens each intent on his own gain, come what may to the others.

In the renewal of vision that may complete the experience of suffering innocently borne – at least innocent in terms of the individual's private life, for none of us is absolutely innocent of the world's stain and contagion – there may be a spontaneous outflow of forgiveness to those who have perpetrated the crime. Thus there have been occasions in which victims of prison camp terror have, before their death, been able to forgive all those who hurt them, and this not in a spirit of moral superiority but one of humble gratitude: had it not been for the wicked action of the persecutors, there would have been no experience of communal love which transcended anything that the world could give in terms of riches, power and recognition. The experience of this superhuman love – by which I mean a love beyond that which one individual can bestow on another in the course of everyday life, inasmuch as it is private and discriminating – was the zenith and ultimate meaning of their existence, and also their mode of forgiving their torturers. In this light we can begin to understand Jesus' almost unattainable demands in the Sermon on the Mount: "Do not set yourself against the man who wrongs you. If someone slaps you on the right cheek, turn and offer him your left . . . Love your enemies and pray for your persecutors" (Matthew 5:39 and 44). Jesus goes on to remind his audience that only so can they be God's children, for God makes his sun and rain available for good and bad alike. We have to love everyone, irrespective of their attitude towards us. There must be no limit to our goodness, so that our very being becomes akin to God. Such an injunction is beyond realization until we remember that Jesus Christ is the effulgence of God's splendour and the stamp of God's very being (Hebrews 1:3). But how Jesus the man retains the effulgence and remains the image of God is a mystery to us until we have traversed the impenetrable dark wilderness of divine ignorance.

In the horror of suffering unjustly inflicted but uncomplainingly borne, an experience of true selfhood emerges out of the darkness. There is a gradual dissolution of the barriers of personality, and the individual attains an identity with his suffering companions. Eventually this identity expands to embrace the entire created order: its life becomes the one life and its being the true being of each individual. A freedom is suddenly known that is unrelated to material affluence; it is a freedom of the spirit of man that roams unfettered in the limitless expanse of eternity. As Heraclitus said, "You can never find out the boundaries of the soul, so deep are they." There is, in fact, no boundary of the individual soul; its depth reaches out to the soul of every creature, to the very soul of creation, and its height taps the Holy Spirit universally and eternally. And so it comes about when the man in the street, who aspires to no special spiritual knowledge or religious commitment, is in contact with a source of human sanctity, as the witless pupil and the master together traverse the barren, featureless plateau of unremitting suffering, the vision of the unenlightened one is illuminated with spiritual radiance, the very uncreated light of God, and he begins to see the path ahead for the first time in his life. It leads to the unknown region where God is to be found. The newly-fledged aspirant is lifted above the fear of death to an existence that contains within itself a new perspective of reality.

But what of the many who move aimlessly on the bare plateau, filled with hatred and seething with resentment? Their vision is clouded by emotional turbulence. They are not able to let go. They cannot surrender themselves and therefore remain closed to an existence beyond the bounds of human suffering. Indeed, suffering, however induced, brings with it seething anger and resentment. How could a loving God allow such injustice to occur, whether the pain is physical or mental, individual or communal? The person who is diverted along the path of recrimination soon finds himself in an enclosed circuit that magnifies the force of his anguish, providing no spark of relief nor any resolution of the difficulty. As much suffering is produced by an attitude of intransigent rebellion to the circumstances at hand as by those circumstances themselves. In a situation of mortal danger, as in a prison camp where there is communal solidarity in the face of imminent destruction, personal striving for life is expanded to fraternal concern. But if the pain is a solitary experience, like that of Job sitting on an ash-heap and covered with repulsive sores, the ego revolts at the injustice of the situation, and moves around in a vicious circle of anger and frustration. In such a condition, the traditional solutions based on Scripture or the world's wisdom serve to irritate the victim rather than strengthen him for onward confrontation with the forces of darkness. The hope is that light will eventually break through the obscurity as the plateau is explored and claimed with trust, care and patience in the face of continuing evil. In the end the core of obscurity is to be mastered and its gloom dispelled.

In fact it is the unyielding attitude of the victim that prevents light penetrating the darkness. The more he fights the sea of misfortunes, the more they close in on him. The more he tries to break loose from the prison, the more securely do its walls surround him. Pure intellectual analysis of the problem soon founders on the rock of incomprehensibility. And a gradually enveloping fatigue takes over the scene; at last the victim can rest in the darkness. Only then can his sense of grievance, his implacable resentment and his subterranean fear be relinquished. Then the light of hope, a light issuing forth from the depth of the soul, can cast some meaning and illuminate some direction in the further journey of the sufferer. It is noteworthy that only when the theological arguments of Job and his comforters came to an end, when silence was at last restored, did God come directly in a vision to Job. It was indeed something more than a vision, which by its nature has elements of separateness about it; it was rather an experience of union in which the deepest secrets of creation were imparted to Job. The silence of rest, the same silence that follows the distribution of the elements of the Eucharist to the congregation, brought the reasoning mind and the turbulent emotions to a halt. And then God could make his presence felt. Though he is always there, we are all too seldom available to receive him because our awareness is distracted with emotional turmoil of one type or another.

When the human mind turns back to the simple trust of a little child at rest, then alone can purpose be divined, and all the pain seen to be an essential part of the person's progress to a liberty that owes nothing to material circumstances. In the sleep of the bruised victim, healing of the damaged personality can proceed; a new person emerges as a phoenix from the debris of past suffering. When this process can take place within the context of the suffering community, a new type of society is being born into the sleeping world. Thus it was with the early Christian community before personal acquisitiveness cast its shadow and obliterated the sun of righteousness, with its warm rays of charity and selflessness. Indeed, too rapid a relief from spiritual travail can allow the old Adam to re-assert itself as the fleshpots of the past cast their enticing shadows once again. Even the children of Israel, in the journey through the wilderness to the Promised Land, were tempted time and again to yearn after their past life in Egypt. Once, however, one is on the healing journey of suffering, a return to the past becomes inconceivable; a forward passage into the unknown region is alone possible, even when its blackness is total, with no light to promise future illumination. The light of which I speak is the light of reason; the light of spiritual perception is always present though increasingly faint according to the spirituality of the victim. This is paradoxical, since one would assume a truly spiritual person would be closer to that light than a mere beginner on the way. But, in fact, the person attaining sanctity has to dispense even with his intuitive knowledge as part of his journey to the ultimate light, a light that is more like darkness to most of us. But, in fact, it is the darkness that one experiences when one gazes directly into a source of intense illumination. As we read in Scripture, no one can see God directly and remain alive. He would in effect be consumed in the uncreated energies of the Creator. But none of this is apparent to the victim in his journey onwards.

The important lesson we all have to learn in our life on earth is to be true to ourselves. This is the meaning of integrity. We have to shed all pretence, including the comfortable covering of propriety that we value so highly. This propriety is not so much an outer attitude of morality as the reputation we enjoy in the company of our peers. It may, especially in our currently permissive society, be an attitude of antinomianism, of direct rejection of the traditional values that sustain society, so that we assume the role of rebel against the moral order, just as easily as that of conformist rectitude. Thus Job had to shed the image of a wise man full of charity, and become a critic of the very moral order he had previously sustained, before he could see the light of God. He did not reject that morality so much as explore its foundations: what he discovered both confirmed its necessity and extended its range in a way that the previous teachers of wisdom in the Old Testament could scarcely have imagined. It showed that our life on earth is a school of spiritual training based on obedience to the Spirit of God within us, and a movement of the chastened soul beyond the world of punishment and reward to an experience of eternity in the present moment. Once personal suffering can be seen in this light it becomes not only tolerable but also filled with hope of ultimate perfection, of practising the way of life that Christ lays down in his teaching and demonstrates in his ministry.

No worst, there is none. Pitched past pitch of grief,
More pangs will, schooled at forepangs, wilder wring.
Comforters, where, where is your comforting?
Mary, mother of us, where is your relief?
My cries heave, herds-long; huddle in a main, a chief
Woe, world-sorrow; on an age-old anvil wince and
sing—
Then lull, then leave off. Fury had shrieked "No ling-
ering! Let me be fell: force I must be brief".

O the mind, mind has mountains; cliffs of fall
Frightful, sheer, no-man-fathomed. Hold them cheap
May who ne'er hung there. Nor does long our small
Durance deal with that steep or deep. Here! creep,
Wretch, under a comfort serves in a whirlwind: all
Life death does end and each day dies with sleep.

No Worst, There is None
by G. M. Hopkins

4

The Failing Light: The Heroism of Affliction

In the trial of suffering so far considered, the pain has been illuminated by the inner radiance of hope. The divine presence which enlightens us all has, if anything, been allowed to shine even more brightly than is usual, because the tawdry glitter of the world has excluded itself in disgust (rather as Jesus' disciples ran away from him when he was betrayed), and the unsullied glow of the divine indwelling is left in sole occupation. In this way intense suffering, especially endured in the company of others in the same plight, can evoke a response of loving forgiveness that lies above mortal conception. For the first time in a victim's life the impress of divinity may be imparted to him, and he may respond in a loving sacrifice of such a magnitude that Jesus' all but impossible commandments to love our enemies and pray for our persecutors become real and practicable. As Jesus taught, for men this is impossible but for God all things are possible. God works, in our little world, primarily through the agency of humans. The greatest love is renunciation carried to the acceptance of death for the sake of the beloved who is identified, in the perspective of injustice and cruelty, with the whole created universe, inanimate as well as living.

But there have been some who have been called, in a state of isolation from all human solidarity, into an experience of even greater suffering where the darkness is all but total. Here the light of God's presence appears to be obliterated; indeed, its very existence becomes increasingly problematic up to the point where the very notion of a meaning to existence appears a terrible delusion. God appears finally to be no more, indeed never has been except in the imagination of the believer, where he has been conjured up to fill the gap of intolerable meaninglessness. A raging whirlpool of destruction, of blank extinction, is all that remains.

The experience is known, at least to some extent, by the person aspiring to truth, who prefers the walk in the cold desert to an ascent to the skies of delight by way of escapist meditation techniques. These promise, and indeed may induce, an experience of bliss, but soon this dissolves in the harsh daylight of mundane disorder. The way of the desert, like the wilderness into which Jesus was led by the Holy Spirit after his baptism by John, is cold and forbidding, but its end is the vision of God for those who persist through all trials and dangers. The Psalmist has at all times a particularly intimate relationship with God, who assumes a strongly personal character, albeit in a presence that far transcends finite description, even to the extent of bearing a name that can identify it. Thus the Psalmist can plead directly with the Almighty to show his hand at once in defence of his chosen people. Sometimes the attitude is one of confession, or pleading, or frank irritation at the length of delay in spite of urgent prayers. But there are also portions of the Psalms where terror is expressed at the spectre of impending doom staring the people as directly in the face as the Psalmist confronts the naked void of annihilation. "Thou hast plunged me into the lowest abyss, in dark places, in the depths. Thy wrath rises against me, thou hast turned on me the full force of thy anger. Thou hast taken all my friends far from me, and made me loathsome to them" (Psalm 88:6–8). Again we read, "When the bonds of death held me fast, destructive torrents overtook me, the bonds of Sheol tightened around me, and the snares of death were set to catch me" (Psalm 18:4–5).

A similar type of experience is recounted in the psalm put into Jonah's mouth as he prays in the belly of the great fish sent by God to swallow him, "I thought I was banished from thy sight and should never see the holy temple again. The water about me rose up to my neck; the ocean was closing over me. Weeds twined about my head in the troughs of the mountains; I was sinking into a world whose bars would hold me fast for ever" (Jonah 2:4–6). These terrible experiences are of a darkness more profound than that due to outside circumstances of bereavement, unjust punishment and torture, or even the progressive failure of bodily function that leads to the individual becoming increasingly isolated from the world around him. The darkness is such that the divine presence is not only obliterated from the spiritual intuition of the victim, but its absence is also felt to be contingent on his sinful nature. Eventually all positive meaning to life is felt to be a delusion. In such a state of obfuscation all attempts at living beyond the covetous desire of an animal are felt to be not only futile but actually non-existent. Therefore judgements based on moral values fall into the chaos of despair.

The human at his best lives in response to a hierarchy of values. The foundation is paved by elementary self-interest without which life would be immediately impossible. Then comes his relationship with those close to him in blood ties, conjugal union and everyday employment: the family unit and the working community constitute the walls of his private house. But the roof, if indeed it exists at all as an integral unit, is composed of the slates of higher moral values. The three cardinal ones are, in the Platonic pantheon, beauty, truth and goodness; the Christian revelation would tend to incorporate the third of these in the wider scope of love. Thus at his basest man lives on a purely self-centred sensual level. As he rises in awareness, his mind in its intellectual mode assumes a more dominating position, so that the person views the world in conscious thought apart from himself. The end of this advance is scientific research and technological enterprise. In this state there remains a gaping hiatus between man and the world. The human assumes a purely distant, even disinterested, I-It relationship with all the creatures around him and the earth on which all survive, man and beast alike. But as man grows into the fullness of his identity, which includes an exploration in depth of the unconscious no less than a vertical ascent to mental supremacy, so the spiritual dimension assumes a more insistent place. Man indeed discovers that he lives not only on bread but on the word of the nameless One which alone sustains the world and is the ground of his own true being, which we call the soul. The human occupies an amphibious place in this world: his feet rest firmly on solid ground while his head is in fellowship with the divine presence. And each polarity must be given its full due: a worldliness devoid of spiritual insight finds its end in death and annihilation, whereas a discarnate spirituality effects no change either in the world or in the person himself.

The journey to spiritual mastery, to the vision of God whose illumination transforms all that attain it into something of the divine nature, is a way of renunciation, sacrifice and impoverishment. But the poverty lays one open to the divine impress, and in that contact a new person is born, one who is totally in union with his fellows – and eventually with all living forms that inhabit the world. In this spirit Jesus says, "Blessed are the poor in spirit [those who know their need of God]; the kingdom of heaven is theirs" (Matthew 5:3). Having given themselves without stint to God's service, they attain an instant knowledge of divine reality. This is the end also of human nature, to share in the very being of God (2 Peter 1:4).

But before this visionary end may be attained, something else may also be demanded of the aspiring person: a blinding of the soul so that it loses its erstwhile confident assurance of God's presence. With this apparent disappearance of God comes a doubt about the reality of the spiritual life and the cardinal values on which it rests. All the previous faith seems to be erected on a foundation of pure fantasy, a wish-fulfilling escape from the true facts of life. The inner voice of destruction tells him, "There is no God who cares for the world and its inhabitants. There is no overall meaning or purpose to life which is not terminated in death. Chance at its blindest governs all events. Life itself is a delusion except as a series of interconnected sensual stimuli that keep the body intact for a limited time." In the words of Macbeth, life itself is "but a walking shadow, a poor player that struts and frets his hour upon the stage, and then is heard no more; it is a tale told by an idiot, full of sound and fury, signifying nothing."

Of course, on one level, this is the entrenched view of the rationalist atheist, and it appears to evince no discomfort in him; indeed he appears to exult in it, inasmuch as he can feel that he alone is in charge of his life and is the master of his fate. But, in fact, this metaphysical point of view has an emotional aridity about it; it belongs to the realm of the arrogant intellect rather than that of the human relationship we inhabit day by day, a world peopled by a throng of fellow workers striving inwardly towards some meaning to a life that is darkened by pain and disappointment even at its most fruitful moments. But deep in the core of the soul of even the most arrogant atheist there burns the light of God's presence as a constant assurance of his grace even if its glow is summarily ignored and its warmth excluded from the conscious life. "The light shines on in the dark, and the darkness has never mastered it" (John 1:5).

In contrast to this intellectually based atheism, the loss of God's presence that the spiritual aspirant suffers is of a completely different order. It is the ultimate bereavement, and one that can never be filled with alternative consolations. This is because all alternatives are as nothing compared with the divine reality that has now apparently departed. Everything is consumed in the destroying fire of futility, so that the very cosmos is reduced to the chaos out of which it was created. To the person who has dined at the heavenly table, earthly banquets are not so much inferior as irrelevant apart from their divine source. Furthermore, the absence of the divine love brings with it something far more terrible than mere intellectual doubt, a doubt that would ultimately reduce the aspiring one to the level of the worldly unbeliever. With the failure of the light of God's love comes a terror as the darkness of suffering appears to overwhelm one in its destructive fury. All around is the sheer blackness of non-existence, and yet paradoxically one is more than ever before aware of one's own being as a separate entity. One is trapped in a vortex of ferocious forces, sucked down into an abyss of primeval destruction, whilst one struggles frantically for one's life, calling out piteously to the one who is not there. And yet one remains alive – provided, of course, the temptation to end one's life is resisted, as is usual in the instance of the spiritually advanced person. He knows, even in his panic, that there is no way out except by going resolutely through the raging torrents of hell. The soul is completely bare in the tempest of destruction; it is felt to be like a little furry animal, like a mole. This is the stature of the personal identity, and it reminds one of Dame Julian's vision of the whole creation as a hazel-nut: "Also in this he showed me a little thing, the quantity of a hazel-nut, in the palm of my hand; and it was as round as a ball. I looked thereon with eye of my understanding and thought: What may this be? And he answered generally thus: It is all that is made." She marvelled how it might last, for it could have suddenly disintegrated into nothing, but she was told that it lasts eternally because God loves it. "And so All-thing hath the being by the love of God" (*Revelations of Divine Love*, Chapter 5). However, the fragile, vulnerable soul flinches before the cold wind of hell, and seeks desperately to remain alive.

How different all this appears from the calm,

detached stance of the rationalist! How remote it is from the traditional piety of the conventional believer who prides himself on his orthodoxy! The impeccable taste and propriety of the reasoning faculty and the traditions of religion recede before the naked onslaught of the power who denies life. So did the disciples from the discredited person of their Master. There is no assurance of victory here, and all the solitary victim can do is to keep on his course, dark, unilluminated as it is. We remember Jeremiah complaining to God repeatedly at the hardness of his lot, being persecuted by the very people he had been sent to save from their folly. The prophet is caught between the power of God's command and the resentment of his fellows: God tells him to get on with the work, but offers no word of comfort let alone any material consolation. But the high point in the prophet's life is his description of the new covenant to be written on men's hearts, so that they may know God intimately as an immediate presence, and not merely as a theological abstraction. The world gains from the life of the prophet, but he himself enters a pit of suffering from which he is released only when he dies in captivity in Egypt, whence his rebellious countrymen have carried him in their futile flight from Babylonian power. Could Jeremiah or the fictional Job, possibly constructed on the personality and suffering of the prophet, have understood the cosmic forces against which they were pitted during their pain? All they had was their own integrity and a faith that was completely dark and obscure.

This sequence of spiritual unfoldment is described memorably by St John of the Cross in his book *The Dark Night of the Soul*. In the first night the soul finds increasingly little comfort in the traditional forms of religion, and verbal and mental prayer become stultifying and unreal. The soul is moving towards a more intimate communion with God, one that transcends images. The end is contemplation, which is the foundation of prayer and also its culmination. The unobstructed mind ascends to the heavenly grace in rapt adoration, while the person gives of himself to God in silent devotion. To the traditional believer this apparent repudiation of the outer garb of faith seems like treason, the very workings of the evil one, but the more experienced spiritual director learns, by his own experience as much as by what he gleans from spiritual authorities, to recognize the true night of the soul and to distinguish it from spiritual pride on the one hand and mental apathy on the other. One always has to bear in mind that the higher one ascends to God, the more open one is to demonic assault. The evil one acts not only directly but also through the flaws and weaknesses in our own character. What we take special pride in is, in fact, the Achilles heel of our personality.

And so the lover speaks to the beloved in wordless joy, and discovers that the beloved is the universal Lover of all creation. No joy could be more complete. But then later in the life of the lover may come the second night, in which the very presence of the beloved seems to have evaporated: God is no longer there, and in his place there is a darkness worse than that of total annihilation. This is "the dark night of the spirit", which is the title of the second part of *The Dark Night of the Soul*. The sixth and seventh chapters of this part of the work describe some of the associations of the dark night very clearly; indeed St

John of the Cross speaks of the whole experience as "dark contemplation": "But what the sorrowing soul feels most is the conviction that God has rejected it, and with abhorrence of it cast it into darkness. The thought that God has abandoned it is a piteous and heavy affliction for the soul . . . When this purgative contemplation depresses a man, he feels very vividly indeed the shadow of death, the sighs of death, and the sorrows of hell, all of which reflect the feeling of God's absence, of being chastened and rejected by him, and of being unworthy of him as well as the object of his anger. The soul experiences all this and even more, for now it seems that the affliction will last for ever." He describes a further "excellence" of dark contemplation as another kind of affliction to the soul: this property makes the soul feel within itself its own intimate poverty and misery. He notes also that because of the solitude and desolation the night causes, the person in this state finds neither consolation nor support in any doctrine or spiritual director; though the director may point out many reasons for being comforted on account of the blessings contained in these afflictions, the sufferer cannot believe this: he believes his director says these things because he does not understand him, and does not see what he sees and feels. Instead of consolation he feels deeper sorrow, thinking that the director's doctrine is no remedy for his evil, rather in the same way that an incurably ill person suddenly realizes that all the existing medical authorities are powerless in treating his condition. The state, if it is to be truly efficacious, will last for several years, no matter how intense it may be, although there may be intervals in which the dark contemplation ceases to assail the soul in a purgative mode, and instead shines upon it with loving illumination. Nevertheless, the purgation continues until the soul is absolutely cleansed of lust, until it is devoid of all egoistic desire. Though the soul habitually possesses faith, hope and love, the present awareness of the privation of God and of the afflictions does not permit the person to enjoy the actual blessing and comfort of these three theological virtues.

To this great mystic these formidable inner experiences are part of the divine purification of the soul, so that it may grow, unencumbered with the least trace of egoistical dross, into full union with God; in its innocent nakedness, like that of Adam and Eve before the fall, it can make the final surge of adoration to the beloved, who is God. But the end is hidden from the one who undergoes the privations of hell; at the most he can glimpse its advent from afar as the peace of death falls over him, a presage of the death he, and all of us, are ultimately to experience. A telling instance of this sequence clouded and glorified the final part of the life of St Thérèse of Lisieux, who died of tuberculosis in her twenties. She is remembered especially for the path of spiritual unfolding she demonstrated: "the little way" to God the Father, in which she, with her naked innocence, was the little child. The beloved Fatherhood of God was incarnated, so to speak, in her own father whom she adored, but who, alas, was to suffer a mental breakdown that lasted until his death.

Following this terrible blow Thérèse learnt to identify God as the Father of all, not merely a personal father to her alone. And so she saw his Fatherhood in all the community of the convent, and in him learned to love all the members, difficult as some of them were, as is inevitable in a closed group of people. The little way was one of complete trust in a loving Father, a way that in turn demanded absolute obedience and self-giving to that Father. The ego was given to God, in whom all love resides, from whom all healing flows. But then she entered the dark night: her beloved Father failed her as terribly as had her earthly father. She descended into the pit of annihilation, of panic, of dread of losing her mind in insanity. She experienced "the night of mere non-existence", as she so terribly called it. She shared the table of unbelievers and partook of their bread. But whereas the unbeliever could munch away unconcernedly, she savoured its bitter taste and empty content. She had lost everything, whereas they knew nothing in the first place. The pain continued unabated until the moment of her death, when she was lifted up into an ecstasy and the usual warmth suffused her face once more. She had indeed accompanied her Lord to Gethsemane, and was subsequently to lead many others to him, as she entered the full membership of the Communion of Saints in the life eternal.

In terms of modern psychological understanding, and indeed in the climate of much current theological thought, the dark night of the spirit is a psychopathological state to be treated rather than emulated. Many regard it as essentially a chronic depressive illness, and St John of the Cross has been labelled as merely a depressive, even by some Christians in religious orders. That the dark night of the spirit is a manifestation of severe depression cannot be denied, but is it simply a psychosis? It must be acknowledged that many of the world's great mystics appear to know nothing of it, at least in the terrible intensity described in the literature.

The main features of severe depression are a sense of dereliction and the loss of self-esteem, so that the person feels he is worth nothing. At the same time all the mistakes of the past are enormously inflated, with a corresponding sense of guilt out of all proportion to the misdemeanour recalled. There is intense emotional sensitivity, so that even inoffensive memories evoke a scarcely bearable inner tension. The depressed person feels he is a total failure and attaches all the blame for this on himself. There is also often an inexplicable feeling of anxiety, so that the person cannot relax sufficiently to fall asleep even when he is tired. If he does drop off to sleep, he soon awakens because the level of the sleep is so superficial, the quality so light. When awake, he has great difficulty in falling asleep again, so that he wakes up in the early hours of the morning and remains awake in a state of listless anxiety. The cause of depression is still unknown. There are sometimes hereditary factors, and the condition not infrequently follows some episode of trauma like childbirth, a surgical operation, or a sudden blow to one's expectations. On the other hand, depression may arise spontaneously. It may be intermittent, with normal periods in between; sometimes it has a cyclical periodicity with alternating periods of maniacal elation. This is called manic-depressive psychosis.

Severe depression can often be successfully treated, or at least controlled, by antidepressant drugs; indeed, the discovery of these drugs has been a major landmark in modern psychiatric practice. In the more intractable cases electroconvulsive therapy is very helpful. The psychodynamic view is that depression is a response to long-repressed unconscious anger. Psychotherapy itself is of little avail during the acute phases of the condition, but it may be valuable during the periods of intermission or when there is only a mild disturbance of mood. It cannot be denied though that a number of depressive subjects continue in their suffering indefinitely, unresponsive to all treatment at present available. Their plight is indeed terrible, and some in despair terminate their lives by their own hand. Both the fictional Job and the St Thérèse of real life were tempted, no doubt on more than one occasion, to this course of action. It was their sublime faith in the goodness of life, despite the apparent contradiction in their own situations, that kept them moving onwards to the fulfilment of their vocations.

It can hardly be gainsaid that some great mystics and saints have a personality predisposed to bouts of depression. The course of their spiritual development makes them more rather than less vulnerable to the malign psychic currents that encompass us all, and which, left unchecked, would lead to total destruction of life. Jesus himself was, after his baptism, led into the wilderness by the Holy Spirit, where he was exposed to the gamut of temptations by the evil one – not only for the traditional forty days and nights but for the entire period of his ministry up to the time of his death. We often forget that he, though perfect in his humanity, had to learn in the school of suffering, as we read in Hebrews 5:7-10. This passage further states that he attained a peak of perfection by obedience in that school. Those less intrinsically whole than Jesus will have their special sites of weakness severely tested by the assault of the dark forces. But if they can persist to the end, their very agony will be their badge of honour, in the same way as the wounds of the crucified Christ become our focus of worship as we contemplate the resurrected Lord. The difference between the sufferings of the two Carmelite saints whom we have been considering and that of the average depressive subject is the nobility of bearing of the former and their calm acceptance in the face of indescribably devastating dereliction: no less than their God had been taken away from them. They had moved far beyond mere self-concern to an involvement in the pain of the larger human situation. Therefore we would be ill-advised to dismiss these two saints as merely mentally sick people, an embarrassment to the spiritual life rather than an adornment of it. Their pain has about it something of the agonised love of Christ on the Cross; it makes us aware of dimensions of the human spirit that enrich the whole of mankind. Furthermore, their agony is an inspiring witness for all those who suffer from depression; their dark victory, their sombre triumph, is a focus of living hope in a shoddy world that looks so often for ephemeral entertainment and meretricious glitter to distract it from the facts of life and death.

There is a tendency in some professional circles to label various handicapped people with their afflictions, and then to dismiss their witness as unreliable. In the realm of behavioural and nervous disorders we have, for instance, depression, schizophrenia, phobic states and epilepsy: depressives, schizophrenics, agoraphobics and epileptics can then be summarily categorized and their particular contributions to our understanding of life cavalierly discarded as the effusions of deranged people. In fact, their contributions can be of unique value, in that they may attain insights foreign to the average run of humanity. In much the same way victims of such physical disorders as progressive diabetes, strokes, inoperable cancer, multiple sclerosis and muscular dystrophy not infrequently learn important lessons of patience and endurance as their maladies move towards a terminal state. Their witness may be an inspiration to those who care for them no less than to their relatives, and not a few attain the stature of sanctity as they persist in courage and faith to the end of the course of their disease. Without this challenge they might have remained typically selfish, thoughtless people.

It need hardly be emphasized that no one is called on to endure misery if there is any means at hand for its relief. Self-inflicted suffering is the morbid gesture of a disordered personality, and it is usually ostentatious with theatrical overtones. It seeks to make an effect in order to gain attention and sympathy. It is the pain that resists all agencies of relief which can be a means of growth of the person to the knowledge of God, who in Christ takes on the sins of the whole world. We should listen with attention and respect to everything such an afflicted person tells us about eternal things as he moves on to the destiny in store for all of us.

The wounded surgeon plies the steel
That questions the distempered part;
Beneath the bleeding hands we feel
The sharp compassion of the healer's art
Resolving the enigma of the fever chart.

Our only health is the disease
If we obey the dying nurse
Whose constant care is not to please
But to remind of our, and Adam's curse,
And that, to be restored, our sickness must grow worse.

The whole earth is our hospital
Endowed by the ruined millionaire,
Wherein, if we do well, we shall
Die of the absolute paternal care
That will not leave us, but prevents us everywhere.

The chill ascends from feet to knees,
The fever sings in mental wires.
If to be warmed, then I must freeze
And quake in frigid purgatorial fires
Of which the flame is roses, and the smoke is briars.

The dripping blood our only drink,
The bloody flesh our only food:
In spite of which we like to think
That we are sound, substantial flesh and blood –
Again, in spite of that, we call this Friday good.

from *East Coker* by T.S.Eliot

5

The Passion of Christ: Gethsemane

An aura of disquiet overhung the last week of Jesus'
ministry. In the stark realism of Mark's account there
is first of all the prophetic anointing of Jesus by an
unknown woman. She, and by imputation he also,
was castigated for wasting so much money on a costly
perfume which could so much more profitably have
been spent on feeding the poor. But Jesus understood
the deeper significance of her action: a love that was
preparing his body for the torture ahead of it and the
burial that lay at the end of the passion. It was also
preparing his soul for the dereliction it was to undergo
when even his disciples would separate themselves
from him and he would be regarded as a creature of
vile loathing. It not uncommonly happens that when
we are about to undergo a particularly testing
experience, those closest to us fail utterly, whereas a
stranger may give the word or make the gesture that
strengthens us and lightens the darkness ahead. In
this way our relationships are extended, and those
who have taken us for granted are both exposed in
their superficiality and jolted out of their rut of
complacency to enter a deeper realm of intimacy and
self-knowledge.

The poor, as Jesus remarked, will always be among
us – indeed we are a part of their company – because
they are unaware of their privilege of being human
and therefore do not bestir themselves to fulfil their

potential as children of God. But Jesus was soon to leave this world, not as a lamented saviour but in the form of a rejected false messiah crucified between two common criminals. In the same way beauty and human dignity are not to be sacrificed according to the expedience of the common purse. It is by them above all else that the imagination of the common mind may be lifted to spiritual reality, to the end that people may become more aware of truth. In this way their actions may ascend the scale of values from mere sensual stimulation to a concern with the world and all who live in it. In this way alone can the poor be effectively encountered and their degradation remedied.

And so the love of the one who remains unknown prepares the body and soul of Jesus for the ordeal ahead of him. At the same time one of the Twelve, Judas Iscariot, probably the most intelligent of the apostles, is so disgusted that his already subterranean disapproval of his master flares up into conscious revolt: he betrays him to the chief priests, who already had enough reasons to hate Jesus because of his immeasurably greater spiritual authority and his capacity to see the truth of a situation with unerring accuracy. Jealousy allied to fear is an especially lethal combination, for it convinces those in power of the absolute necessity of eliminating the troublesome person in terms of the public interest; in this concern their naked jealousy can be convincingly presented as pious rectitude.

Then comes the preparation for the Passover meal. The disciples are to seek a man carrying a jar of water, who will show them a large room upstairs set out in readiness for the supper. Water plays an important part in the work of Christ, not only signifying the purification of baptism but also the downpouring of the Holy Spirit. In John 4:13-14, Jesus says that everyone drinking the water from a well will be thirsty once more, but whoever drinks the water that he provides will never suffer thirst again. Indeed, in the miracle attending the marriage at Cana-in-Galilee, Jesus turns water into wine, a symbol of the transformed potency of material things in the hands of the Lord of life. And so the Passover meal is endued with a spiritual potency of a magnitude that is to make its advent the precursor of a new sacrament of redemption of the whole world from darkness to light, from death to resurrection.

During the most fateful meal that has ever been eaten Jesus speaks mysteriously of the one among the disciples who is about to betray him, and all of them turn to him in incredulous concern but there is no explanation. Then comes the momentous institution of the Eucharist, whose mysterious part in the world's redemption is still to be understood. Jesus says that never again shall he drink from the fruit of the vine until the day when he drinks it new in the kingdom of God. He has indeed completed his earthly work; foreboding is aligned with authority, relief with dread. His mastery is established among a small group of disciples who hang on his words, yet no one understands him. His loneliness, always overwhelming despite his constant mixing with all classes and types of people, is now absolute; a gulf of spiritual intuition separates him from all his disciples as he leaves the upper room, with the sound of the great Passover Hymn echoing in his ears, and leads them in the crisp chill to the Mount of Olives.

There he tells them that they will fall from their

faith, for it is written, "I will strike the shepherd down and the sheep will be scattered". But nevertheless he assures them of his later resurrection, after which he will go before them into Galilee. They are all anxious to proclaim their loyalty, none more so than Peter, who nevertheless is told that he will disown Christ on three occasions that very night. And so they reach a place called Gethsemane where Jesus bids them sit, while he takes with him the three closest disciples – Peter, James and John – as he goes further on to pray silently. And then the cosmic battle commences.

At once the calm, melancholy mastery of Jesus, who embraces within himself a humble human frame and the Sonship of God, is enveloped in darkness. He descends precipitous into the void of unseeing chaos out of which the cosmos was created by himself, through whom all things were made. The Lamb of God slain before the foundation of the world – inasmuch as the creation is the form of his perpetual sacrifice, his ceaseless giving of himself for the sustenance of all he has created, the maintenance of the cosmic order for which he is responsible in a perpetuity that proceeds until his final coming in glory – is now cast down to the prince of darkness, so that he may be discountenanced and all his work brought to nothing. And who is this prince from whom the darkness proceeds? He is the created one of God who has used his will perversely to dominate all that is, in order to devour it and make it his own. But in this assimilation to evil intent of all that is, the creation becomes dismembered, destroyed and utterly annihilated. And so the cosmos returns to the chaos out of which it was formed by the self-giving love of God. Jesus descends into the void of annihilation where his mastery and foresight are all submerged and rendered impotent. His very identity is obscured so that he does not know himself in his fullness, while at the same time being excruciatingly aware of his existence. The agony increases as the heart is torn from the body, at least symbolically, as the soul is dragged from the personality that encloses it.

The darkness of the chaos of non-identity is not simply the result of the deprivation of light, the light of understanding and meaning. It is also a powerful and positive force of absolute negation, just as deliberate cruelty is something apart from the removal of love. This would leave a blank indifference, so that the creature would be at the mercy of any harmful outside agency and a helpless victim to its own inherent processes of decay and death. The positive act of cruelty aims at the humiliation of its victim so that it cries out in agony to the God who is not there, and once registering the fact of that absence, begins to curse loudly in its agony and to die. But is God in fact absent? Certainly no apparent trace of him can be detected in the black, foul stench of total chaos, and yet the very malice of the evil one seeking to destroy all that he encounters makes visible the presence of God. For there is no positive action that registers awareness of another creature, no matter how full of hatred that action may be, that does not manifest something of the divine nature. This is why a positive hatred is closer to God than a blank indifference, which is ultimately the most terrible form of denial of love. What I hate I still acknowledge; what I dismiss I leave to the attention of and destruction by the elements of nature. The agony of Jesus in the Garden of Gethsemane embraces both active destructive hatred and an indifference that leads to neglect, isolation and disintegration. Thus evil is, in the end, a complete denial of love, the power that not only heals, but also brings life into the cosmos and promotes its growth to fulfilment.

Did Jesus have any knowledge of all this before the time of his agony? I believe that he did, but essentially on the level of intellectual acceptance, to which was added, no doubt, a strong intuitive insight. Job, after he had been brought low to the point of physical disintegration, admits to his three comforters, "Every terror that haunted me has caught up with me, and all that I feared has come upon me" (Job 3:25). Job was undeniably attached to the things of this world, especially his family and his reputation; the prospect of them being taken away was more than he could bear, until their removal from his life actually happened. Jesus was attached to nothing on a purely personal level, since everything on earth was spiritually his own by virtue of his act of universal creation in the world of eternal value. But he did love his Father in heaven. Indeed, the love of Father and Son in the world of universal creative impulse brings forth the Holy Spirit who is the Lord, the giver of all life. The Creator Spirit enables the Word of God, the Son, to do the eternal creative work, inasmuch as by him all things are made. And yet in the context of Gethsemane even the union of Father and Son is undermined so that, at least on a manifest level, it appears to be broken.

The identity of Jesus is inseparable from that of his Father: "Anyone who has seen me has seen the Father", and again, "I am not myself the source of the words I speak to you; it is the Father who dwells in me doing his own work" (John 14:9 and 10). And now apparently the collaboration is disrupted, the union dissolved. The terror of the Gethsemane experience is not so much the threatened obliteration of the personality and the denial of the integrity of the soul, but the meaninglessness of all existence deprived of the supreme identity which is God. It therefore follows that only a saint can know this most terrible spiritual experience; the taking away of the God of faith and intimate communion so that the person is entirely on his own in an ocean of black meaninglessness and overpowering hostility. Jesus was later to articulate this realization when, on the cross, he cried out, "My God, my God, why hast thou forsaken me?" (Mark 15:34). Now the very fact that this cry is also the first verse of Psalm 22 indicates that the awareness of blinding isolation in a whirling vortex of indrawing forces moving towards total annihilation was not unique to Jesus at Gethsemane. But as the psalm ends on a note of relief and praise to God, so the experience of the common man is fortunately of limited duration. Then there is victory. But how is this victory won in eternity? Who is he that triumphs over the evil of the cosmos, that challenges the terrible indifference that presages total annihilation?

Jesus survives the onslaught of the evil one, who brings all things back to the chaos of meaninglessness, by his power of prayer. This is indicated in Luke's account of the agony especially, where it is stated that angelic forces sustain him in his travail. This is indeed the ultimate test of holiness: to persist in faith when all sources of faith have evaporated and to continue in love when there is apparently total destruction with nothing left to love. In the earnest round of spiritual conversation this sounds clear and laudable, but in the darkness of real life it is tantamount to clinging onto an illusion, to grasping a support that does not exist. And yet the supreme faith based on love causes it to exist.

This may indeed be the basis of what we call a miracle. To collaborate with the known God in the general round of good works is the privilege of the man of virtue. To collaborate when God is no longer there is the vocation of a saint. The progress from virtue to sanctity depends upon a stripping of all intellectually held belief, and a casting of oneself into the unknown. And this sequence cannot, indeed must not, be initiated by a direct act of will, for then the ego would subtly supersede that divine direction. The result would be a self-imposed martyrdom which could disastrously mislead those who follow. The movement to holiness is directed by God, whose burning presence replaces all previously held beliefs with a faith so clamant that it can indeed move mountains. But none of this is visible to the one struggling in the Gethsemane experience; its fruits are available to those who follow rather than to the victim himself. Furthermore, there is the ever-present possibility that the victim may give up the ghost on a mute note of failure. It was not a pre-ordained certainty that the mission of Jesus had to end on a peak of resurrection; he could easily have fallen prey to the temptations of the evil one during any part of his ministry: self-inflation or despair depending on the circumstances that presented themselves in his life. Did not Job's wife tell him to curse God and die? Just as it was Job's sense of perspective and gratitude for all the things granted in the past that bade him persist, so it was Jesus' supreme love of all created things that led him onwards through the blinding chaos of destructive forces to the silent path of death in absolute acceptance.

Why was Jesus' heart ready to break with grief as he descended into Gethsemane? And for what purpose did he bring the three chosen disciples with him? The grief was the immediate effect of the psychic darkness of hell upon him; he felt, and indeed was, one with all who suffer in the anonymous, indifferent hell of dereliction of which physical death is the outer manifestation, at least to those who have not penetrated more deeply into their own inner being and seen the way beyond bodily dissolution to survival of the personality in a broader milieu of eternal life. The psychic darkness is the effect of accumulated sin since the dawn of creation. It is the fodder of the powers of evil intent on dominating the world prior to its destruction. I have little doubt that the prospect of death, an event in store for all who inhabit a physical body, did not itself weigh heavily on Jesus. It was the collective darkness that has to be confronted at the time of death, the accumulation of the world's debris of sinfulness, that descended physically upon him and nearly broke his heart. He is, as St John says, the Lamb of God who takes away the sin of the world (John 1:29). He bears it in his radiant innocence, but the impact is almost too terrible to conceive. The sin cannot be dissipated from a distance; on the contrary, it has to be confronted directly and borne in agony. Only then can it be brought out of the darkness of chaos into the light of God's love where it may be accepted, healed and transfigured. Sin corrupts all that is noble and beautiful, in the same way that dry-rot undermines the structure of a building until its walls collapse and its architecture disintegrates.

The darkness of Gethsemane consists both of the accumulation of sin in the universe and the power of the forces of evil who batten on all that is fine and upright, as they did on the body of Jesus itself. But the helpless body, filled with the power of love, can redeem all that was lost and bring light into the void of darkness. The three disciples were there initially to support their Master in the uncharted depths to which he was obliged to descend. Human solidarity is a wonderful support in times of spiritual darkness, but how many people do we know who can remain with us in a terrible descent into hell? Certainly the three with Jesus were of no manifest help, though perhaps their bodily presence was of some strange reassurance to him even when his sight was obliterated in the darkness of corporate evil, of cosmic despair. Though the disciples thought highly of themselves during the period of Jesus' triumphant ministry, they had no spiritual depth to stay awake and support him in his period of agony. Their consciousness was as yet entirely self-centred: the spirit is always willing, but its work in our life is to raise up the flesh from its primeval animal coarseness and sensual demands to a spiritual height that can see beyond the limits of self-gratification to world service. An earnest prayer is brought to the notice of the dull, uncomprehending disciples: that they may not be put to the test, that they may, at least at that moment, be spared the ordeal. This clause has been included in the more composite Lord's Prayer, that we may not be led into the temptation of either self-inflation or despair, until we are at least ready for the supreme trial: few there are that can accompany a soul on its journey along the road to Gethsemane. Soon the disciples are to know Gethsemane in their own dejection as their Master is killed, and they have to proceed onwards with whatever inner sight they still can call upon, whatever faith they can muster.

Paradoxically, we can often see more clearly in the darkness than in the light, because the inner eye of the soul is activated by the cloud of unknowing when the superficial eye of reason is dimmed. As God said to Samuel in the affair of the anointing of David, "Men judge by appearances but the Lord judges by the heart". It is the consciousness of the heart that distinguishes spiritual vision from intellectual judgement. The ultimate prayer of Jesus comes indeed from his heart, "Abba, Father, all things are possible to thee; take this cup away from me. Yet not what I will, but what thou wilt." This prayer of petition finds a climax of belief in obedience to a Father who has effectively hidden himself in the darkness that surrounds his Son. As Job said in a not altogether dissimilar circumstance, "If he would slay me, I should not hesitate; I should still argue my cause to his face" (Job 13:15). Even the apparently inevitable death of the holy one will not dampen his trust in God's providence, even the providence of a God who seems to have absented himself from the world he has created. This is the depth of the experience of Gethsemane. It transcends the intellect and enters the heart of existence.

6

The Passion of Christ: The Way of the Cross

When Jesus had ironically for the third time chided his disciples for their somnolence in the face of their Master's terrible suffering, he told them to arouse themselves; the Son of Man was about to be betrayed to sinful men. They had to go forward to encounter naked evil. Almost at once a crowd of ruffians appeared, with Judas Iscariot at their head. He had already arranged a sign with the crowd: "The man I kiss is your man; seize him and get him away safely." And so he greeted Jesus with a kiss, and the crowd seized him and held him fast.

The deeper significance of this episode is obscure, yet challenging. In all probability Jesus was well known to most of the crowd, sent by the chief priests, lawyers and leaders. Judas' final identification of his Master would seem to be peculiarly otiose – indeed, in Luke's account of the betrayal the chief priests, officers of the temple guard and the elders are identified as the crowd. Probably they formed part of it. Perhaps the Judas kiss had a deeper, more sinister effect, after the Gethsemane episode, of draining what was left of Jesus' charismatic power. When he was in the full flowering of his ministry no task was too great for him, but with the betrayal his powers seemed to recede; in his weak helplessness he appeared no more impressive than any criminal arraigned before the officers of the law. A not altogether dissimilar episode occurs in the Book of Judges, when Delilah coaxes from her exhausted husband, Samson, the secret of his superhuman strength, namely his Nazirite consecration to God, of which his unshaven head is a sacrament. Once his wicked wife has the locks of the hair of his head shaven off, his strength drains away, leaving him as weak as any other man. At the end of this magnificent story Samson's strength gradually returns during his captivity to the Philistines, who blind him and make sport of his powerlessness: they have already destroyed the sight of both eyes, but the hair of his head slowly regrows. In a vow of extreme dedication to God, his strength returns as the Philistines hold him prisoner in their temple and mock his impotence; his great strength is restored, and in a final mighty movement he brings down the entire temple, thereby killing more Philistines in this calamity than he did during his entire ministry. The primitive, vengeful aspect of this narrative quite rightly offends our deeper sensitivities, but the mechanism underlying it is still worthy of our attention. It stresses how those close to us in a personal relationship can either fill us with extra strength or else deplete us of it. The effect depends on their character as well as their intentions. In this respect the disciples were of little use to Jesus during his passion.

There is an immediate response among the bystanders, one of whom draws his sword and wounds the High Priest's servant. In the account of Luke Jesus restrains this show of violence and heals the servant's wounded ear, but apart from this episode his complete powerlessness is obvious, so that as he is arrested, all the disciples desert him and run away.

Jesus is manhandled by the crowd, who bring him into the High Priest's house where he is minutely cross-examined. Jesus' silence in the face of the various conflicting accusations made against him is both impressive and disconcerting to foe and friend alike, reminding us of the prophecy. "He was afflicted, he submitted to be struck down and did not open his mouth; he was led like a sheep to the slaughter, like a ewe that is dumb before the shearers" (Isaiah 53:7). Finally, according to Mark, the High Priest questions Jesus directly about his messiahship, and Jesus affirms that he is indeed the Messiah and that they will see the Son of Man seated at the right hand of God and coming with the clouds of heaven. To the whole assembly this is absolute blasphemy, and a unanimous verdict of guilt is proclaimed and a sentence of death demanded. How dare any man claim parity with God! Almost to prove the falsity of Jesus' claim some of them blindfold him, and while striking and spitting on him, challenge him to play the prophet and identify his assailants. Whilst this nasty game is proceeding, Jesus' disciples are well out of range, and Peter denies on three occasions ever having known the man. On a deeper level he spoke more truly than he knew, for although he had been a constant companion of the Master for three years, he had never been able to penetrate the outer appearance to reach the inner man. When the inner man was revealed in all his frailty and powerlessness, neither Peter nor any other of his disciples recognized him. He was, in fact, too much like them all in their own weakness to be of much support and comfort. They were much more concerned about their own well-being than in the safety of the one to whom they owed everything. He is now the light that has failed, the prophet discountenanced by the religious authorities and shown up to be no better than the other false messiahs who preceded him.

"As soon as morning came, the chief priests, having made their plan with the elders and lawyers in full council, put Jesus in chains; then they had him led away and handed him over to Pilate" (Mark 15:1). Pilate's cross-examination in the presence of the chief priests evokes little response from Jesus, who keeps silence, the silence both of weakness and of sepulchral strength. Pilate can find nothing wrong in Jesus sufficient to warrant punishment, let alone death, and offers to release him whom he calls "the king of the Jews". He realized that malice rather than justice lay behind the condemnation of Jesus. Nevertheless the crowd, incited by the priests, had portrayed Christ as a dangerous agitator to Pilate, who alone had the power to authorize a person's death by crucifixion. In Luke's account, Pilate hands Jesus over to King Herod's jurisdiction, but the King again gets no response from Jesus and returns him contemptuously to the Roman governor. In the end Pilate capitulates and gives Jesus over to his enemies for crucifixion after he has had him flogged. In the more extended account in John's gospel, Jesus claims a kingdom that does not belong to this world. He says he was born and came into the world to bear witness to the truth, and all who are not deaf to truth listen to his voice. But Pilate asks, "What is truth?" Francis Bacon has accused him of not staying for an answer; indeed, for two thousand years the world has remained ignorant because it has not been silent enough to hear that truth. The truth refers back to the nature of God as pure spirit and the necessity of worshipping him in spirit and in truth (John 4:23). Anyone who has seen Christ in the emptiness of agony knows God as spirit, a knowledge terrifying to man until he too has become nothing, even as Christ was during the period of his passion.

And so the outer humiliation and inner torture of Jesus proceed. The psychic hell he encountered as the ground of selfish human existence in Gethsemane is now exteriorized in the open world of direct human relationships. Its terror is to some extent diluted by its overt character; other people are also involved in it in comparison with the isolation of the remorseless psychic fury of Gethsemane. The antagonism of the masses adds its content to the psychic burden of Jesus' ordeal, but it is at least tangible and therefore more easily confronted. When the Master entered Jerusalem only a few days earlier he was acclaimed by the crowds of disciples: "Blessings on him who comes in the name of the Lord! Peace in heaven, glory to the highest heaven" (Luke 19:36-38). Now rejection alone confronts him. His lack of resistance in the face of his arrest proved conclusively that he was not a political messiah, one who would liberate Israel from the tyranny of Roman occupation. Indeed, his kingdom was not of this world, where the masses are enclosed in their restricted concerns.

If Jesus had experienced overt betrayal and rejection by those he loved, the populace felt equally betrayed by him on whom so much expectation had been fastened. He soon assumes the comforting role of scapegoat for their disappointment, incited as they are by their jealous, malicious religious leaders, who see in Jesus a spiritual authority that eclipses their merely ecclesiastical power to enforce the law. As St Paul says, "The qualification we have comes by God; it is he who has qualified us to dispense his new covenant – a covenant expressed not in a written document, but in a spiritual bond; for the written law condemns to death, but the Spirit gives life" (2 Corinthians 3:6). The written law was a light of God at the time of Moses, but it had become a sepulchre of human darkness by the time of Christ, a tragedy of all spiritual things when they become the possession of men, who imprison their contents and make use of them to their own selfish advantage. The one who bursts open the tomb of selfish complicity to the light of God's Spirit is an inveterate enemy of the religious establishment. Herein lies the tragedy of the spiritual life, the manifest triumph of the forces of evil, the victory of darkness over light. History shows us that the victory does come to an end, but not until enormous devastation has been wrought. And it seems to be inevitable that darkness must have its say, at least for a period. It is indeed a moment of triumph when Jesus is divested of his executive powers. He assumes the role of scapegoat as a source of failure, and now he can be tortured in the name of religious orthodoxy. The crowds follow blindly in the wake of the evil intentions of the ruling party, a course of events all too familiar when a despotic regime establishes itself on the ruins of a more humane predecessor. In such situations there are few more immediately pleasurable experiences than hitting a good man when he is down on the ground, alone and bleeding. And so Jesus descends precipitously into the darkness of vilification, unaided by any visible agency.

Once the death penalty has been proclaimed, the soldiers take Jesus into the courtyard, dress him in purple and place a plaited crown of thorns on his head. They salute him contemptuously as king of the Jews, then beat him about the head with a cane, spit on him, and pay mock homage to him, while the blood from the thorns beaten into his scalp trickles down his face. Once they have had their sport, they strip Jesus of his purple robe and dress him once more in his own clothes. And then comes the procession to the place of crucifixion. Jesus falls under the weight of the cross he has to bear, and a man called Simon, from Cyrene, is pressed into service to carry it for him. They bring him to the place called Golgotha or Calvary, which means the place of a skull, where he is fastened to the cross. He is stripped of his clothes, which are shared among the soldiers, who cast lots for individual garments. So the bleeding Master is nailed to his cross. He refuses the palliation afforded by drugged wine. There he is secured, exposed and naked, for all around him to gaze upon, to point to in scorn, and to ridicule. Behold the man called by Pilate the king of the Jews: tormented in soul, agonized in body, reviled by those around him, yet isolated from any human contact. The Son of Man who is also the Son of God has indeed taken on himself the full intensity of the human situation: pain of body and the horror of mental anguish, the light of hope slowly receding from him as he enters the unknown region where even God is hidden from spiritual sight. The human tragedy of meaninglessness is assumed as Jesus moves into ever-deepening darkness. Made in God's image, man sinks day by day into the slime of heedless submission to the forces of darkness. And so did Jeremiah, the sacrificial lamb of Jewish prophecy, when he was thrown into the muddy pit by King Zedekiah's functionaries, who equated Jeremiah's prophecy of doom, in the coming encounter with the Babylonian invaders, with treason against the Judean state. It was only the loyal compassion of a eunuch that saved the prophet by having him raised out of the pit before he was completely sunk in the mud to die of starvation (Jeremiah 38:1-13). There was ultimate relief for Jeremiah, at least in that appalling situation, though his life was one long chapter of suffering from the time of his call, after which he was ostracized even by those close to him, to his death, carried away by renegades to Egypt, where they hoped vainly to escape Babylonian invasion. But the justice of God can never be evaded.

The agony of human life is a compound of bodily pain, mental distress and emotional isolation even when in the closest company of one's peers. We are born lonely, for there is something of the soul that is sacred. It can never be satisfied with merely human company, for it remains unfulfilled, restless and strangely empty until it has attained the vision of God. The loneliness we all share, however oblivious of it we may be in the immediate thrust of workaday life, is unassuaged until we know God, who alone is constant and real. Jesus knows his Father intimately, and so can remain at peace even when the world is at war against him. Nevertheless, the steadfast calm of Jesus even under the pressure of human revulsion and the more terrible underlying psychic onslaught is severely tested, as he cries out those terrible words of absolute dereliction, "My God, my God, why have you forsaken me?" He is in the situation of Jeremiah in the muddy pit, but there is no one present to haul him out to safety. As we have previously noted, the words of the desolate Christ are the first verse of Psalm 22, but there is no reason to believe that he continued to the end of that psalm, which ends on a note of relief and victory after a terrible ordeal. But there is no victory for Jesus on the cross, at least in the eyes of passers-by who taunt his impotence, or the chief priests and lawyers, winking slyly to one another as they challenge the Son of God to descend from the cross and to save himself, instead of simply helping other people. If he would do that then they too would believe in him! When Samson was taunted by the Philistine nobility in their temple, God gave him strength to destroy them all; when Jesus calls to his Father there is complete silence. Even the two criminals crucified on either side of Jesus taunt him, although in Luke's softened account of the crucifixion one of them does repent and acknowledge his holiness.

After Jesus' terrible cry of desolation, wilfully misinterpreted by some of the bystanders as a call of help to Elijah, there is another loud cry. And then Jesus dies. The first fruits of his victory are made manifest by a centurion in attendance: the entire episode had impressed him beyond measure, and he was able to affirm that Jesus, unlike the false messiahs who had come to a similar end, was truly a Son of God. A number of women were also present watching from a distance, amongst whom were three closely involved in the ministry of Jesus. In John's account, one of them was his own mother, the blessed virgin Mary. Of all who had known Jesus, these women seem to have been the only ones to sustain him in his agony. This support the three chosen disciples were totally incapable of affording at Gethsemane, while during the crucifixion they were, according to the record, all discreetly absent from the scene. The deep-felt spiritual support those humble women must have given to the afflicted Christ cannot be emphasized enough. "They also serve who only stand and wait", wrote John Milton at the end of a sonnet dedicated to his own blindness. As we wait in powerless love, so the Holy Spirit flows from us as an unending source of healing, and the strength afforded those in need is out of all proportion to our apparent inactivity. This is the secret of intercessory prayer, which alone can heal the hearts of fearful men in authority and of women consumed in destructive emotional entanglements.

It is reported that the curtain of the temple was torn in two from top to bottom: the separation of sacred from profane was now abolished. All flow into a common stream of God's forgiving love, and a new era of human relationships is about to begin. All is now sacred when dedicated to God in love and to our fellow creatures in service. But how has all this been attained? The detailed account of events leading up to Jesus' death on the cross – easily available in all four gospels, each with its own special emphasis, seeing, as it were, an event from slightly different points of vantage – has been rehearsed here in order to show his deepening humiliation, his definitive entry into the realms of human agony on a gigantic scale of physical and mental torture, and his total engulfment in the darkness of unknowing as the tragedy unfolds. The word "unknowing" is used deliberately: he entered blindly into what was to befall him. He had no outer control; his strength lay alone in what he had within himself, and this was stretched almost to breaking-point by the time death had ended this part of his agony. The state of unknowing differs vastly from mere agnosticism, which is a comfortable attitude of mind in an intellectual debate about ultimate reality. It lacks, however, a living contact with personal strife that we all have to meet as part of our mortal existence. After all, annihilation at death could be regarded, in terms of pure reason, as preferable to the struggle for life that all creatures seem inherently equipped to experience – a focus of deep faith, more certain than intellectual proof, strives desperately for a manifestation of the meaning that it inwardly divines. It drives us on inexorably to the end of the unknown region, which is the vision of God.

When we consider the sufferings of Christ there is a tendency, less common nowadays than in the past, to become so emotionally involved with the person of Jesus that we fail to place his witness in the larger arena of workaday life. Personal devotion would have been quite repugnant to the man Jesus, who saw his own ministry as depending entirely on the power vouchsafed him by his Father. He is indeed the way, the truth and the life, and no one comes to the Father except by him (John 14:6). The explanation of this exclusive claim is that he, in the frame of a simple man, takes on the burden of sin of the entire world, encounters all mortal darkness, whether physical, mental or psychical finally assuming the role of a deluded prophet who fails in his attempt to save the world from the inroads and defilement of sin. Though without sin – by which is meant a character that seeks its own advantage without regard for the well-being of those around it, and indeed often to their detriment – he assumes the form of a criminal on the cross of human vindictiveness, onto whom all sin can be projected and all hatred deposited. He was led like a sheep to the slaughter, but on his back the full suffering of creation is laid. As he dies, so does the darkness of sin attain illumination; it attains a knowledge of forgiveness as it bursts open to receive love. It is transfigured into something of the nature of eternal service. By his scourging the world is healed, inasmuch as every circumstance of human degradation is now lifted up to God, forgiven and restored.

The sufferings of the crucified Christ are remembered each Good Friday. In some churches the sacred Liturgy is recited, in others the traditional Seven Last Words from the Cross form the basis of an impassioned recital of the agony undergone by the Master, who bears the sins of all the world in his racked body. Jesus was crucified at nine in the morning, and at midday a darkness fell over all the land. It lasted three hours, when Jesus uttered his terrible cry of desolation and then died. But more important than all this is the understanding that Jesus, in essence, fully embraced the agony common to all mankind. Some of us die in torture in prison camps, others in bed after an illness of variable duration and suffering. Some die shockingly in aircraft or road traffic accidents, others are killed in the course of their duty in defending their country against hostile assault. Jesus could not, in the frame of a single person, have experienced all these different modes of death, but he did know of the emotional anguish and psychic darkness that underlies them all. In other words, he imbibed the terror that we all experience when we register the imminence of death in our lives. It is this numbing terror rather than the actual mode of dying that is our greatest ordeal, the test of our ultimate faith. In this respect there are many who impress us with their complete equanimity to the fact of death; they have a clear intellectual conviction of what they may expect after death – or indeed that there is nothing to expect at all except extinction – and so can face the event calmly in their own minds. But when they are confronted with the actual threat, their comfortable composure is apt to evaporate, and they experience a terrible inner void not unlike that known to other, less assured, people. In other words, rational conviction is completely obliterated by the fact of imminent dissolution. There is nothing despicable about this: Jesus himself, though on at least three occasions he predicted to his disciples the sequence of his passion, death and resurrection, was nearly overwhelmed by the intensity of the suffering he had to bear. At that stage the intellectual assurance of ultimate victory was completely overshadowed by the darkness of evil that encompassed him. Once this ordeal has been faced in quiet helplessness, one can let the divine power take charge of what remains of one's life on earth, and be carried along the escalator of transition with the trust of a little child.

Thus the latter of the seven traditional words from the cross are less despairing: "I thirst"; "It is accomplished"; and finally, "Father, into thy hands I commit my spirit". This last sentence is a quotation of Psalm 31 verse 5, and is the ultimate test of all our lives on earth: what sort of spirit do we then commit to God? We do not know; Jesus' own life and ministry seemed, in the limited view of Good Friday, to be a terrible failure, to be the delusion of yet another false messiah. Time was to tell the true stature of Jesus' life, as it does of our infinitely less distinguished lives too. As the soul breaks loose from the moorings of the body to which it was firmly attached during active life in the world, so it is less concerned about the things of this world – its injustice, cruelty and humiliation – and more in harmony with the things of eternity, the chief of which is love. So Jesus commences his work on the cross with a gesture of complete forgiveness for those who, in their ignorance, strive to kill him. He ends on a note of dark acceptance, as much agnostic as comforting; and this is the honest attitude of all who are facing the nearness of death: "I have faith; help me where faith falls short" (Mark 9:24). Had Jesus had absolute knowledge of his resurrection, his witness among us ordinary mortals would have been merely theatrical, for he would have possessed that assurance to which we lesser ones grope in faith. But he too groped, and in a darkness infinitely denser than anything we could endure because of his extreme psychic sensitivity. He could have failed – otherwise the incarnation would not have embraced a totally free will. But he persisted to the end of the road, which led downwards to the least of his many brethren. The Holy Spirit works for the release of all prisoners, and not merely the charismatic effusions of the elect.

7

The Descent to the Dead

After Jesus died, Joseph of Arimathaea claimed the body from Pilate. He took him down from the cross, and wrapped him in a linen sheet, laid him in a tomb cut out of the rock, and then rolled a stone against the entrance. The place was noted by some women followers of Jesus.

And then there was a complete silence for two days – the remainder of the Friday and the whole Sabbath Saturday. The matter was closed, and a shock of emptiness, a cold wind of finality, confronted the community. "Without protection, without justice, he was taken away; and who gave a thought to his fate, how he was cut off from the world of living men, stricken to the death for my people's transgression? He was assigned a grave with the wicked, a burial-place among the refuse of mankind, though he had done no violence and spoken no word of treachery" (Isaiah 53:8-9). Admittedly the grave of Jesus was not situated in such degraded precincts, but the immediate memory of the man was associated with such company. Once a stone is dropped into a lake it disappears from view, and its site of entry into the depths is marked by a series of ripples that spread out and are soon dissipated in the expanse of water. So likewise does the life of Christ fade out on those two silent days, when the world had to return to its routine workings in the absence of a cherished leader and inspired teacher. But where was the presence of Jesus during this period of dark silence, of unuttered despair? He was in the immediate afterlife state, and descending not merely to the dead but to the silent, desolate region which is called hell.

In the infernal realm there are to be found the souls of the derelict, those who have wasted their lives in self-indulgence, those who have contributed nothing to the good of their fellow creatures, those who have battened on society and acted destructively in their personal relationships. They are out in the cold, isolated and in despair, beyond reach of any help because they are closed in on themselves, unable and unwilling to give anything of themselves even to the extent of welcoming another creature to their inner being. But even more terrible than those derelict entities is the malign psychic current that circulates around them. It is like a howling wind on a frosty night, penetrating the bones to the very marrow, like a pungent odour permeating the depths of the psyche. The darkness of desolation experienced on a temporal level by those suffering from depression in our world is the atmosphere into which the entities in hell move and exist. Indeed, this darkness is an emanation of undiluted evil, merited by those enclosed in the inferno of isolation, and assumed by the saintly ones who experience the dark night of the spirit as part of their work for the redemption of the world.

The dead whom Jesus visited comprised the sluggish, unaware ones, those who mill around in the blue night of death in the noiseless tumult of the anguished, who groan in hopeless terror at the onslaughts of destructive power wielded by the demonic forces. These control the realm of hell, and seek assiduously to extend their domain by infiltrating the ranks of the uncommitted, those of little faith who move irresolutely at the behest of any plausible outside force. There is, furthermore, a psychic osmosis between the living and the dead; indeed, there is only one life, and what we call death is, in fact, a transition zone, a gateway to a further experience of consciousness, one in which bodily limitation is at an end and the essence of the soul laid bare in its unclouded sensitivity. Jesus promised the penitent criminal crucified alongside him a sharing of paradise that very day, and yet after his death he descended to the nether regions instead of ascending to the heavenly ones. In fact Jesus was in a state of paradisical joy after his death, paradise in this respect being pictured as an oasis of fertility in the midst of a desert, comparable to the world of Adam and Eve before they fell into sin and separation by forfeiting the unending knowledge of God by their selfish desire for personal advancement. Jesus' personal suffering no doubt ended with his noble death on the cross, after which a peace of holiness came upon him. In that state of suffused joy he descended into the world of the dead as an action of outflowing love to its denizens; he also proclaimed his sovereignty over that region, so often forgotten and condemned to darkness.

St Paul, in the famous passage of Philippians 2:5-11, traces the descent of Christ, though divine, into the nothingness of the human condition, assuming the nature of a slave, humbling himself even to the obedience of accepting death on a cross. Therefore God has raised him to the heights, bestowing on him a name above all names, that at the name of Jesus every knee shall bow – in heaven, on earth, and in the depths – and every tongue confess the Lordship of Jesus Christ, to the glory of God the Father. But the glorious name of Jesus is not given as an honorary title; it is attained by Jesus' intimate involvement in all aspects of the creation. By him were all things made – as the creative Word of the Father – yet he is also the Lamb of God sacrificed before the foundation of the world. He is both the resurrected Lord and the perpetual victim of the world's neglect and cruelty. He will remain in an agony of cosmic proportion until the end of the world, until all the creation comes to accept his love of its own accord, until the wills of all rational creatures turn in obedience to him by whom they all were fashioned.

The work of Jesus among the dead to whom he descends in humble solicitude is variously interpreted by the believer. To some he is a messenger, an angel in actual presence, who brings the news of salvation to the saints who preceded him – for instance, the prophets of the Old Testament era. He frees them by bestowing on them the light of God's full grace. To others he is portrayed as a mighty warrior grappling with the powers of darkness and utterly vanquishing them to their destruction, a process popularly described as the harrowing of hell. It was a prominent theme in popular medieval devotion. His power triumphs over all evil, and brings a new dispensation to the inhabitants of the underworld. This approach appeals mightily to those who exult in the concept of spiritual warfare ending in the victory of the forces of light over those of darkness, so that good completely annihilates evil. While this is unexceptionable enough as a general principle, it is all too easily transposed without modification into the world we inhabit, and the attitude it engenders can be divisive and dangerously judgemental. In this way all those who deviate from an accepted pattern of piety, who question the assumptions of an established religion, are associated with the works of darkness, the company of demonic entities that govern the material world: those who are not explicitly with us are against us. The outcome of such a categorical attitude is a demand for justice that finds its end in persecution and excommunication. Separated from the body of the faithful, the dissident elements can be eradicated in slow, calculated steps and then completely destroyed.

This is indeed the poisonous fruit of the alignment of spiritual authority with physical power. The history of the world's major religions bears a sad testimony of worldly self-seeking at different periods; they have all at times succumbed to the temptation of colluding with prevailing political forces in an attempt to establish their own domination of the local scene. The plausible intention of asserting its God-given influence not only excuses this collaboration but actually justifies it, at least in their own eyes. True spiritual authority walks humbly with the unrighteous world in the hope of transfiguring it into something of the measure of Christ. Once it falls into the temptation of lowering its sights to that of the world around it, it becomes as debased as that world to the extent of attaining a parity with the forces of evil. Thus Jesus mixed with the whole range of human nature during his ministry on earth: all those who came to him in openness of heart he released from the shackles of material desire to an encounter with their true nature as sons of God. But he himself remained uncorrupted despite the moral disorder around him, because the

Spirit of God infused him and flowed from him as a spring inside him, welling up to eternal life, as is described in John 4:14. The power of the Holy Spirit prevents a person falling victim to the temptations of the world, the flesh and the devil – in this context the three are in fact one. The powers of this world, especially political power, act insidiously to debase the aspiration of the human spirit until it becomes so involved with the forces of desire that it loses the vision of eternal life. Well did Jesus rebuke James and John when they volunteered to call down fire, in the manner of Elijah, on the people of a Samaritan village who would not receive them on their way to Jerusalem (Luke 9:51-56). Conversion that is real responds through love to God, a love that banishes all fear, even the fear of personal annihilation. In other words, love acts even to its own eclipse: as is said by St John Baptist in regard to his relationship with Jesus, "As he grows greater, I must grow less" (John 3:30).

This was Jesus' great work in the world of the dead: to give of himself to the faceless multitude so that they might know the first promise of resurrection. He claimed his own domain by entering it at its lowest level, in a way previously shown in the washing of the feet of the disciples shortly before the agony commenced in its full intensity. He came in love to embrace all those who would receive him, whether in the world of matter or in the world beyond the portal of death. This world is shadowy and yet in psychic continuity with our past aspirations, our present attitudes, and our future endeavours. Love cannot inflict itself on another; it can simply give itself in humble generosity. He stands at the door of the soul and knocks; if anyone hears his voice and opens the door, he will come in and sit down to supper with him. But the invitation is ours, not his. Furthermore, the hell that Jesus enters in pure love is not confined to the afterlife. On the contrary, it is a very real ingredient of our present situation until the time comes when we are sufficiently aware to appreciate him and acknowledge him in thankfulness.

He is the nameless presence alongside all those who are suddenly cast down into the darkness of loneliness and foreboding as disaster strikes in everyday life: the person suddenly bereaved of that which made his life tolerable, indeed meaningful, and especially the one suddenly afflicted by incapacitating illness. After the initial shock has been faced and absorbed, the spark of hope flickers inwardly. It leads us to a faith which enables us to act according to the instructions of a source beyond our own cognition. He is that spark within that ignites the hope; he is the faith that leads us on the uncharted path through darkness to ultimate light, a light far more radiant than the light of reason at its most brilliant. Faith acts, whereas belief rests comfortably in an intellectual environment. In this life we do indeed "see through a glass darkly", recognizing only puzzling reflections in a mirror, but when we act according to his light within us, we are moving to that time when we shall see face to face. Christ is the master of our darkness, just as he is also the master of the underworld. What was previously the domain of the powers of darkness has now been decisively claimed by the forces of light. This does not mean that God has at any time abdicated his dominion of the infernal realms, but that, in identifying himself with all that suffers in them, he asserts an authority that includes even the demonic forces that so often appear to rule our world no less than the lower regions of the world of the life to come.

His dominion is not a triumphal one, nor are the forces of darkness summarily banished. His kingdom is not of this world that we know only too well; it is a heavenly kingdom. He brings heaven to earth, light to darkness, by his perpetual self-sacrifice. Just as the bread of the Eucharist is broken into small fragments to nourish all the communicants, so he is eternally broken, to the end that all who receive him may perceive the light of God even when they are immersed in the cloud of darkness. Christ, in other words, comes to his own – who are all created things, the dark no less than the light – as a lover, not a conqueror. He does not lay siege to the powers of darkness until they fall, as did Jerusalem and the Holy Temple to the Babylonians in the time of Jeremiah. He offers himself as the perpetual eucharistic sacrifice, whose broken body and flowing blood nourish all who will receive him, to the world of becoming until that far-off day when every blade of grass will have been redeemed, every recalcitrant heart turned into an organ of flesh that flows out in love to all its fellows. This vision looks in hope to the salvation of all the universe; it asserts that nothing God has made will ever be finally rejected; it proclaims that the presence of God in even the most evil person or lethal organism will in the end be its means of redemption from the chaos of disintegration and annihilation. The terrible division between the blessed and the damned, defined unequivocally in many of the sayings of Jesus, so that the latter are doomed to eternal rejection, is not denied by this statement: on a short-term basis the law of cause and effect acts relentlessly and cannot be altered to suit ourselves. But the love of the crucified, degraded Christ acts even to transcend this cosmic law, the moral expression of which is mirrored in the Law of the Old Testament. The man Jesus who uttered the words of terrible judgement when he was alive in the flesh has himself grown to a greater perfection through the experience of suffering and death: Gethsemane and Calvary have opened even his compassion to the full tragedy of the human situation. No one is ultimately beyond healing, so much are we all parts of one body. This was the great work that God the Son – in the body of a humble, almost anonymous, first-century Palestinian Jew – came to achieve.

Jesus was indeed a great spiritual teacher, but his words form part of an ongoing tradition that is called "the ageless wisdom" or "the perennial philosophy". What marks him out as distinct from the other holy men of human history is his participation in the darkness of hell, and his power to transfigure even that darkness into the light of sanctity by the action of pure love. But just as the light has never been mastered by the darkness, so the darkness has never allowed itself to be illuminated by the light. The cosmic conflict proceeds; whoever uses force in the battle on the side of the light simply increases the intensity of the darkness. Love alone can penetrate the dense barrier of darkness and bring a ray of light into it as an earnest of its transfiguration. For God created the dark as well as the light, "I am the Lord, there is no other; I make the light, I create darkness, author alike of prosperity and trouble. I, the Lord, do all these things" (Isaiah 45:7). God is the first cause of all that is, but by the freedom of choice, a consequence of free will, he has given his rational creatures the ability to use or misuse the creation. The element of choice illuminates the allegory of the Fall in Genesis 3, and is a constant accompaniment of all subsequent human striving – the human, no doubt, sharing a psychic osmosis with the intermediate angelic hierarchy with its fallen demonic counterpart. Nevertheless, the ultimate responsibility for all things is God's, and on this realization we can rest securely in his love, knowing that he is not remote from his creation. The witness of the world's saints throughout the ages underlines this divine concern, which in Jesus is made fully incarnate and indeed available to all modalities of experience, whether in this world or the life beyond death. God in Christ bore the whole human situation, and in him there is a promise of healing for all those who are open to his undemanding love.

The situation is beautifully expressed in George Herbert's poem *Love*:

Love bade me welcome; yet my soul drew back,
   Guilty of dust and sin.
But quick-eyed Love, observing me grow slack
   From my first entrance in,
Drew nearer to me, sweetly questioning
   If I lack'd anything.
"A guest", I answere'd, "worthy to be here."
   Love said, "You shall be he".
"I, the unkind, ungrateful? Ah, my dear,
   I cannot look on Thee."
Love took my hand and smiling did reply,
   "Who made the eyes but I?"
"Truth, Lord; but I have marr'd them: let my shame

Go where it doth deserve."

"And know you not," says Love, "Who bore the blame?"

"My dear, then I will serve."

"You must sit down," says Love, "and taste my meat."

So I did sit and eat.

In another context William Blake in his poem *The Little Black Boy* also sees the primacy of love as the testing experience:

Look at the rising sun: there God does live,
  And gives His light, and gives His heat away,
And flowers and trees and beasts and men receive
  Comfort in morning, joy in the noonday.

And we are put on earth a little space,
  That we may learn to bear the beams of love;
And these black bodies and this sunburnt face
  Are but a cloud, and like a shady grove.

For when our souls have learn'd the heat to bear,
  The cloud will vanish, we shall hear His voice,
Saying, "Come out from the grove, my love and care,
  And round my golden tent like lambs rejoice".

This love acts to bring us to perfection, and in so doing condemns itself to a death which is also the gateway to a life that knows no ending. But it is a hard thing to bear the love of God: our innate pride sheers off from the divine encounter, for we are not prepared to lay ourselves completely open to a force beyond our understanding. What can be understood can to some measure be controlled, and in the life of the present world this alone we will accept. But in the ultimate concerns of life and death our control slips unless it is infused by a God-given strength, a strength Jesus drew on during the blinding period of his passion. Like the guest in George Herbert's poem we too are overwhelmed by our unwholesomeness, that so easily assumes the magnitude of a total worthlessness in the face of God. And yet this attitude is paradoxically a morbid self-indulgence, an inverted form of egoism. We have in fact to assume the stature of a little child, oblivious of considerations both of worth and power, before God's kingdom opens up to receive us. At this juncture Jesus shows us the way of divine darkness in the face of the mystery of an all-powerful God who mourns perpetually for his fallen children, seeking to reach and redeem them with a love that never fails but can never assert itself against their will.

The Father mourns the agony of the Son, not only during the event of the passion, but throughout the entire history of creation: the Son, by whom all things are made, gives himself in unremitting love to his creatures; they merely trample on the pearls he bestows and then turn to tear him to pieces. This apparently never-ending sequence is not so much one of sheer malice as of uncomprehending unawareness, of negligent carelessness. It is like the child who dismembers the insect, torments the domestic pets, tramples on the flowers of the garden, almost to demonstrate his mastery over them and to assert his strength. Later in life, in the silent recollection of a dark night, with the winds of tragedy blowing in at the windows of his little house, he may reflect ruefully on his destructiveness, but then it is too late to undo the damage caused in the past. Yet did not the One on the cross cry out, "Father, forgive them, they do not know what they are doing" (Luke 23:34)! God's anguish for his creatures, the pathos he feels for them in their wilful destructiveness that has spoiled the natural order, that has thwarted the magnificent future he had in mind for them, is movingly expressed in much of the Old Testament narrative. The Book of Hosea especially expounds the theme of God's love for his unfaithful people – a love that can never wane, for all true love is eternal – relating how he punishes them by the ultimate law of cause and effect in order to inculcate in them the spirit of faithfulness, how they repent half-heartedly only to apostasize once more, and how in the end they are promised forgiveness as a gift of pure mercy.

In the parable of the Wicked Husbandmen (Mark 12:1-9), the father sends his beloved son to collect his share of the produce from the intransigent tenants, who have repeatedly manhandled the servants he had previously despatched to carry out this work, the servants in this context being the prophets whom the chosen people disregarded and assaulted. But instead of honouring the son and obeying his injunction, they conspire to kill him so that they themselves may obtain the inheritance. This is the measure of gratitude God is shown by those he has created – and yet the work of creation must continue. The Son in his pain seems to be separated from his Father by a limitless gulf: on the cross he cries out in agony to the God who appears to have left him in the lurch in his moment of greatest need. His terrible cry is more than a purely personal lament, a heartrending plea for relief from his suffering. It is also a pathetic yearning that the eyes of the hostile crowd may be opened, that their blind incomprehension may give way to an understanding of the nature of his mission, that they too may break through the limitation of selfishness and enter the spiritual realm of growth and consecration to God. This is the revelation of the love of God, eternally present but at this fateful juncture of history purposely hidden from the view even of the Son. God is no longer merely an outside presence who controls the world but can be called on in prayer. In this climactic moment of human understanding the previous image is extended and a new relationship with God established in the heart of mankind. He is now fully incarnate in the soul as an interior power of sanctification and not simply one that can be called upon from afar by a prayer of convenience when the necessity for his intervention arises. The newly attained understanding knows God as a presence of fragile weakness that gives itself in love unfailingly and perpetually to all that lives. And yet in this apparent helplessness, that refuses to effect a single action of self-centred relief, there lies a strength that may bring about a transfiguration of the entire world. Where the power of coercion has failed, the vulnerability of love has found a way into the heart of the cold world, the soul of an unheeding humanity. We may see in a fresh light the answer given to St Paul when his condition remained unhealed, "My grace is all you need; power comes to its full strength in weakness" (2 Corinthians 12:9). How many incurably ill people have learned this eternal lesson, this ultimate truth!

8

The Peace of God

"On the third day he rose again in accordance with the Scriptures." This pivotal clause in the Nicene Creed describes the resurrection of Jesus and by application points the way of transcendence to be experienced by all in affliction who do not lose faith, who proceed by the unknown way to the destination, at once totally obscure and also the light of the soul. The end of the impenetrable gloom – a darkness inaccessible to the rational mind – is the light of God in whom there is no darkness at all. In the preceding darkness all guile has been shed, all dross discarded, and a new creature emerges from the chaos of hell, one that can confront the uncreated energy of God and be protected from its consuming heat and blinding light.

And yet, in a way barely comprehensible, the new creature is identical with what was originally formed, innocent, chaste and exquisitely sensitive, but now the thick accretion of sin has been transformed by love and integrated into the risen body. When Jesus showed himself to those close to him, who had been able to respond to his love, albeit in small measure only during the period of his incarnation, he was scarcely recognizable at first sight. Mary Magdalene mistook him for a gardener until he addressed her in a characteristic word of greeting. The disciples on the Emmaus road encountered him as an illumined stranger until he broke bread with them and said the blessing. Indeed, all the disciples needed to have their eyes opened before they were capable of receiving their beloved, unknown Master, now known in love for the first time in their association with him. He was the same person and yet strangely new. The physical body had been transmuted into spiritual radiance, and the anguish of the past emotional strain eased into a presence of calm benediction. His own delight in appearing to his friends in a form completely new to human experience is brought out in the freedom and spontaneity of his manifestation among them. His attitude is one of amazed joy. He had come through to a glory that even he could not fully have anticipated, a glory that did not emit physical power or even overt spiritual authority, but rather a sense of living presence, of work well done, a rest in the Father and then renewed effort in another dimension of reality – for he can never be at rest for long while there is suffering around him, whose round is cosmic in scope. He did not need to prove, let alone assert, himself nor to reprove his disciples for their lack of faith; his very presence among them did this. He did not show himself to the mighty in the land, those who had conspired to kill him. Had he done so, he might well have shocked them into repentance, but then they would have abused this also for their own selfish ends when the ripples in the water of time had eased out into bland memory. They were instead to learn the truth in their own time, as a heart opened to God in love but not as a body driven by the threat of punishment. And the process is not complete twenty centuries after the event of the resurrection. His was a visitation of forgiveness not power, of love not coercion.

And so it is with all those who have passed through the valley of darkness and arrived intact on the other side, breathless, almost speechless, and yet strangely composed; they are at last at peace with themselves and with the world. The attrition wrought by suffering has released them from dependence on all earthly ties, even the solidarity of those whom they sincerely believed they loved but who simply did not have the strength to accompany them in their moment of greatest need, the hour of ultimate trial, the pit of the valley of desolation. "The Spirit is willing, but the flesh is weak" (Mark 14:38). In the instance of the person who has traversed this darkness, the flesh is no longer weak, for it has been transfigured into something of the spiritual body we are all in process of fashioning for the life beyond death, even while we are busily involved in the things of this world. This is our glimpse of the resurrection that was fully accomplished in the life of Jesus Christ.

As the victim emerges in sombre celebration from the grave of human understanding, the eclipse of worldly honours and ephemeral delights, so there is neither recrimination nor triumph but only a deep sense of relief that wells up into wordless joy. He is invested in a bare nothing that incorporates everything; he recognizes the Deity as the supreme No-Thing, and is at peace. He no longer grasps at any worldly prize, for in himself he contains the cosmos. This sequence is especially well illustrated in the resurrection of Job from the darkness of incomprehensible woe to the awesome felicity of God's presence. He did not understand why he had suffered so cruelly and perhaps never attained this knowledge, but in the divine presence he attained a state of greater illumination, one in which his previous pain was as a fleeting shadow in the light of God's eternal day. Indeed, when we can glimpse the radiance of God's providence in the universe, our personal afflictions take on the magnitude of a little child's tears as it is carried summarily to bed when it would prefer to stay awake to play with its brothers and sisters. "I know thou canst do all things and that no purpose is beyond thee. But I have spoken of great things which I have not understood, things too wonderful for me to know. I knew of thee then only by report, but now I see thee with my own eyes. Therefore I melt away; I repent in dust and ashes" (Job 42:2-6). Although in fact Job had much about which to complain, much to resent, nevertheless, caught in the divine mystery, he assumes something of that mystery himself. He attains a serenity previously unknown to him during his days of affluence, philanthropy and punctilious religious observance, when he, above all else, prized his reputation and cherished his children. No worldly concern assumed overwhelming importance any more, because the divine presence encompassed everything and transfigured it into an essence of eternal value.

The peace of God that passes all human understanding is an atmosphere of holy communion in which every creature moves beyond its solitary identity to give of itself in unsparing service for the entire community. The sacramental life is then completely fulfilled in the divine fellowship of the present moment. Pain has given way to reconciliation, the demand for recompense to a burning charity for all that lives, and the fear of personal loss to a spontaneous self-giving for the sake of the neighbour, who includes all that lives. A mutual sharing of resources now blesses the whole community whose centre is the Father, whose periphery is the Son, and the energizing force that fosters relationships on all levels from the divine to the secular, the Holy Spirit. The evil of the world, a world subject to the corrupting influence of powers and entities far beyond the grasp of the reasoning mind but incarnated in human relationships by the divided consciousness that is part of the inheritance of unredeemed mankind, has in a glorious way been transcended. And this transcendence has not simply bypassed the corrupting currents that so often govern the world. It has incorporated them in the goodness that lies at the heart of all searching relationships, growing in painful truth to the self-giving of real love. And so a divine compassion, an overflowing forgiveness, pervades the entire living scene. God was indeed in Christ reconciling the world to himself, no longer holding men's misdeeds against them (2 Corinthians 5:19), and in this presence the darkness of cosmic evil has been submerged in the abyss of God's compassion. From the depths of the divine being it has emerged new and untainted. Now at last the enormous demands of Christ can be, indeed have been, fulfilled: do not set yourself against the man who wrongs you . . . love your enemies and pray for your persecutors . . . there must be no limit to your goodness as your Heavenly Father's goodness has no bounds (Matthew 5:38-48). The mystery of the naked evil of Gethsemane that has its lesser counterparts in every human situation of incurable illness, impenetrable depression, heartless crime, vicious persecution or cosmic disaster, is that it finds its resolution and healing in the process of life itself, when that life is completely open in childlike trust to the Holy Spirit, the Lord and giver of all life. The Gethsemane experience is the ultimate transmuter of evil inasmuch as evil itself can do no harm in the person who accepts it unconditionally, without resentment and in a state of innocent love. That is the chaste love of the humble person who gives of himself to his fellows without so much as being aware of his great gift. He also takes on himself unconditionally his share of the world's darkness, and by his simple incorruptibility transfigures it into a thing of holiness.

The return from the dead is an attainment of a second simplicity, common to all the saints of the world's spiritual traditions, a realization of the supremacy of reconciliation glimpsed by the martyrs as they move beyond their individual allegiance to embrace a corporate unity even with those who persecute them. The new life of the sanctified, who are the ordinary people of any age that have passed from the darkness of imprisoning despair to the light of God's love by their own courage and self-sacrifice, is a presage of the new creation promised by God at the end of time (Revelation 21: 1-5). The restoration is no longer sombre and forbidding, as is mortal existence even at its most prosperous, inasmuch as decay and death lie at its end. It is open and full of joy; it sparkles and bubbles over with a sense of the ridiculous at the pomposity of all human aspirations, no matter how proper in tone and correct in content, when they are not liberally seasoned with an awareness of the essential humour that underlies all events. The human earnestness contrasts as a dark pall with the unpredictable radiance of the divine providence that embraces all creation, whether good or bad. For in this moment of truth the mystical understanding of God as the coincidence of opposites dawns upon the newly born creature. God is indeed beyond all concepts, even those of good and evil. In him all things co-inhere; though he transcends the cosmos, yet he is the indwelling power in every creature, and he has also walked beside the creature along its own path of death and resurrection in the person of Jesus Christ. That which defeats the naked intellect of the thinker explodes like a flash of brilliant light on the one who has passed through death to the life that knows no end. And this life is none other than the previous life of the person, but now fully experienced in unclouded awareness for the first time.

And so the justifiably rebellious Job is given a kindly, though illuminating, lesson in natural history by God, who reveals himself in his magisterial glory when the theological impotence of all the disputants has reduced them to silence. God shows himself not only as the creator of the world but also as one who is intimately involved in the welfare of his creatures – not only the brilliant human being but also the brute force of nature and its manifold animals. All these are as much subject to the divine compassion as is mankind. One can, if one reads the text with the simplicity of a small child, hardly avoid smiling as the prodigies of the various animals are called to Job's mind: the ostrich, the horse, the hawk, the vulture, the whale (or hippopotamus) in its enormous size, the crocodile in its ferocity and impregnability. Each passes before his entranced gaze in one mighty cavalcade directed by God. The divine pity disports itself prodigally with a universal, celestial love, while the human plays his little part in the world's economy before he too is put to rest like a tired but spirited child.

The final chapter of the Book of Job has often been criticized as something of an anticlimax: after the magnificent theophany in which God reveals to Job something of the enormous mystery of creation, Job returns once more to earth. He gains wealth and cattle while a new family takes the place of the one that perished. Indeed, Job's final state of affairs seems, if anything, to be even more satisfactory than the earlier period of his career. But this view is, I believe, to misunderstand the essential nature of his restoration of resources and personal rehabilitation among his compatriots. When anyone has come through an experience that has, quite literally, stripped from him all the previous landmarks whereby he could recognize his place in the community, his perspective is immensely broadened. His priorities, his sense of values, undergo a radical reappraisal. No longer is he seduced by possessions, for he has seen beyond the fascination of private ownership. He ceases to care for worldly honours, nor do even personal relationships of an intimate character ensnare him. To be sure, human relationships are the staple of our life on earth, but even they, at their most blissful, can imprison us in a web of complacency which is unceremoniously cut away by the inroads of decay and death. They are to be seen, in the mature light of attrition and resurrection, as transient episodes of great beauty which, if cherished in nobility of service, will lead us to the greater relationship with all that lives, a relationship that can never end, since God and not the personal beloved is its centre.

In other words, our little term of ownership is seen in its more enduring form as stewardship of resources for the benefit of all those around us, just as family ties school us for the time when, as Jesus taught, all who do the will of God are our ultimate family. We hope that in the fullness of time this family will be all-inclusive. The death of the beloved, once it has been borne with courage, will find its sequel in a greater concern for our neighbour, in whose familiar features we may suddenly see the face of the loved one, just as the disciples on the road to Emmaus saw the person of Jesus in the stranger they encountered on the way. To those who have not been stripped of all they had previously regarded as essential to their lives, such a radical broadening of concern is inconceivable; to those who have had their lives miraculously restored, what they have left of themselves is no longer personal property but communal resources. This is the transpersonal life that Jesus shows his disciples as he moves among them in his resurrected form. Mary Magdalene can no longer cling to him in a uniquely personal relationship, nor can the disciples on the Emmaus road detain him indefinitely. His scope of action is altogether wider now, until the time of his ascension to the Father. After that event his is a truly cosmic presence available universally as a light of transforming radiance.

And so, to return to the restored Job, one can feel a peace about him that was not present at the beginning of this wonderful story. Then he clung to his wealth, his reputation and his children, and there was something even about his piety, sincere as it was, that worshipped a far-off God of inflexible justice, who had to be appeased at all times, especially when Job's

children celebrated and perhaps said or did something
improper. After his suffering, Job's relationship with
God is altogether easier: the distant potentate of
justice and power is now a friend in the spiritual
atmosphere around him. God still transcends all
human definition since he is not encompassed in the
cosmos he has created, and yet the divine presence lies
within Job closer than his own soul. In Christ,
furthermore, God also walks alongside us in our
travail, and probably Job became aware of this when
he had returned from his own private death to
participate in the new life of eternity that still
embraces the world of creatures. But now the
creatures, including the humans among them, are part
of the divine providence into which Job can throw
himself in joyous abandon. Jesus tells us to set our
mind on God's kingdom and his justice before all else,
and then all the things of this world, for which we
strive so obsessively and fight so obdurately in
ordinary consciousness, will come to us as well
(Matthew 6:33). One feels that Job has arrived
exhausted but entire at this knowledge, and can now
relax in all his new friends, letting them pursue their
own existence and simply flowing out in benediction
to all life. Thus the spiritual person bestows blessings
quite spontaneously, as a presage of the Holy
Communion, in which we receive a joint blessing from
the Author of all creation. All life is a sacrament of
God's grace, and as we move in love to all we
encounter, so the sacrament attains a universal
fulfilment.

It seems a strange progress in a person's life to move
from the innocence of childhood to the murky depths
of adult sensuality and greed, only to be brought low

by one misfortune or another in order to rediscover something of the chastity that was long ago discarded. The path of integrity seems to require nothing less than a total renunciation of all worldly favours. The first part of man's descent into the grime of common existence was poignantly lamented by William Wordsworth in his "Ode on Intimations of Immortality" from *Recollections of Early Childhood*.

> Our birth is but a sleep and a forgetting;
> The Soul that rises with us, our life's Star,
>   Hath had elsewhere its setting,
>   And cometh from afar;
>   Not in entire forgetfulness,
>   And not in utter nakedness,
> But trailing clouds of glory do we come
>   From God, who is our home:
> Heaven lies about us in our infancy!
> Shades of the prison-house begin to close
>   Upon the growing Boy,
> But he beholds the light, and whence it flows,
>   He sees it in his joy;
> The Youth, who daily farther from the east
>   Must travel, still is Nature's priest,
>   And by the vision splendid
>   Is on his way attended;
> At length the Man perceives it die away,
> And fade into the light of common day.

It seems that the hard school of adult competitiveness and insidious temptation to corruption of moral values, as far from the manifest light of God as a riotous public house is from the sanctuary of a church, plays its part in developing the individual character, in a way that the bliss of childhood purity could not provide. This is the darker meaning of incarnation, both our own and that of the Son of God. Even Adam and Eve came to a stern self-knowledge and an awe of God that was remote from their experience during their idyllic existence in paradise, only when they had fallen outside it. The golden youth, more prevalent no doubt in the spacious era of the early romantics like Wordsworth than in the chaotic, undisciplined world we now inhabit, can still breathe the atmosphere of holiness as a gift. Later on, when he descends into the grime and dirt of common manhood, he has to provide this atmosphere from his own resources, as Jesus did among the common people with whom he consorted. But whereas Jesus adorned any society he encountered, no matter how morally unclean it might be, the golden youth is rather more likely to be corrupted by his environment than to edify it. The wages of sin are indeed death, if not immediate mortal dissolution then at least the destruction of the entire edifice of security that the heedless person has built around himself. In the suffering and isolation that ensue, the person, like the Prodigal Son, may come to himself once more. It is indeed the same self that he knew as an innocent child, the soul no less of a unique individual, but now that self has come of age, and can start to do the work for which it was called at the time of its conception. In the call of Jeremiah, God said, "Before I formed you in the womb I knew you for my own; before you were born I consecrated you, I appointed you a prophet to the nations" (Jeremiah 1:4-5). I believe that some vocation lies at the heart of all human existence, and it may be that the Prodigal Son type of experience is necessary for many of us not only to discern the true from the false but also to learn humility and thus be able to enter into the lives of our many suffering fellows. The humble person does not know everything, and can learn from even the most unpromising people.

Just as Job returns to his little world a stronger, wiser man, so does the Prodigal Son come home to the estate he had left in the precipitate, thoughtless haste of youth. But now both of them can appreciate their good fortune with mature vision and a peace of benediction. By contrast, the older brother of the Prodigal Son, despite his virtue and industry, has been oblivious of the magnitude of God's grace. The saddest part of this great parable is his father's gentle remonstrance at his unloving attitude towards his brother who has come home, as it were, from the dead, "My boy, you are always with me, and everything I have is yours." So many of us can become caught up with our work, possessions and personal relationships to the extent of being imprisoned in them instead of enjoying them. In the same way obsessive piety can obscure from us the face of the living God; the history of religious persecution is a terrible testimony to this tendency to worship religion rather than God, to love the set dogmas of our faith to the extent of hating our brethren. Once we have passed through our own valley, as dark as death, we can, in the words of Psalm 23, relinquish all fear of evil, for the Lord himself is now manifestly with us, an unfailing support day by day. He always was with us, but until then we were not with him, since the glamour of the world had captivated our attention and blinded our spiritual sight. When we come together with God in a mature, responsible relationship, we regain the vision of our heavenly lineage and can start the homeward journey in a joyous faith that far transcends the unaided reason.

In this state of quiet benediction, we no longer need to justify ourselves, our faith or the providence of God. The intellectual proofs (and disproofs) of a meaning behind the creative principle, indeed the very existence of such a principle as opposed to blind chance, become increasingly irrelevant to our inner stability. Our faith no longer hangs on the support afforded by great names or fresh scientific evidence, nor is it disturbed when the names depart and the evidence is questioned by the agnostic faction. This does not mean that the intellect is contemptuously dismissed, but simply that a higher principle of understanding has been revealed to us, one on which all other modes of human knowledge ultimately depend. This principle is the Deity himself, who is known, as *The Cloud of Unknowing* tells us, by love but not by thought. The state of contemplation transcends all discursive thought and enters that breathless silence in which all human knowledge is illuminated with a purpose whose nature is love. And so we no longer have to dispute with others so as to prove our particular point. Instead, we can embrace all people with love, learning from them instead of merely arguing with them. At last we can attain the height of the divine commandment: love your enemies and pray for your persecutors. At last we can grasp Jesus' supreme commandment, old enough indeed in the annals of spirituality but now new in its blazing intensity: "Love one another; as I have loved you, so you are to love one another" (John 13:34).

And so the end of this strange life of ours appears to

be the full actualization of the soul, always illumined by the Holy Spirit immanent in its holiest place, the spirit, but so often clouded by the cares of the world and the emotional turmoil that flows from them. To know who we are and what we are to become is the purpose of our brief, but very significant, sojourn on earth. And yet we always knew this in the depths of the soul, but ran away from the place of peace to be diverted by the world's vanity. Nevertheless we, like the Prodigal Son, shall return to our own being – which is also the kingdom of God – enlightened and radiant with love. As T.S.Eliot puts it at the end of *Little Gidding*:

We shall not cease from exploration
And the end of all our exploring
Will be to arrive where we started
And know the place for the first time.
Through the unknown, remembered gate.
When the last of earth left to discover
Is that which was the beginning;
At the source of the longest river
The voice of the hidden waterfall
And the children in the apple-tree
Not known, because not looked for
But heard, half-heard, in the stillness
Between two waves of the sea.
Quick now, here, now, always –
A condition of complete simplicity
(Costing not less than everything)
And all shall be well, and
All manner of thing shall be well
When the tongues of flames are in-folded
Into the crowned knot of fire
And the fire and rose are one.

When I read these familiar lines, my mind recalls with poignancy Beethoven's last quartet, how the deep suffering of the penultimate slow movement is consummated in the joyful simplicity of the finale – not a simplicity of craftsmanship, but one of mood. It evokes in me the vision of little children playing in the Elysian Fields, with no thought except the immediate present which is also eternity. And so a lifetime of hardship, frustration and deep inner suffering, but illuminated by divine inspiration, attains its apogee in a paean of childlike innocence. There is no triumphant conclusion here, at least in terms of the world's bombast and show, but instead a return to the paradisical state of Adam and Eve before they fell from grace. But whereas our two allegorical ancestors were unaware of the bliss in which they lived, the resurrected person not only appreciates that bliss but also adds his unique contribution to it. Joy and love unite in service which works towards the healing of all that is out of alignment, that cannot face the reality of God. "As in Adam all men die, so in Christ all will be brought to life" (1 Corinthians 15:22).

We started this study by considering how the sun fills us with hope and resolution when its warm rays play upon our skin and brighten our sight, and how its decline darkens our inner vision no less than the outer one, so that we retire into a state of pensive regret. But when we are born to reality, we no longer depend on the sun to encourage us. The true sun is radiant within us, the divine presence radiating the uncreated energies of God. "And the city had no need of sun or moon to shine upon it; for the glory of God gave it light, and its lamp was the Lamb. By this light shall the nations walk, and the kings of the earth shall bring into it all their splendour. The gates of the city shall never be shut by day – and there will be no night" (Revelation 21:23-24).

Epilogue

The sequence of a person's rebirth to the image of God, in which he was originally fashioned but has nevertheless to attain as a willed act through his own experience on earth, has an important consequence: inner integrity that pays allegiance to nothing else than the highest within him.

The temptations that beset each of us day by day can no more be evaded than could Christ claim exemption from the temptations of the evil one when he was led into the wilderness by the Holy Spirit after the humble acceptance of John's baptism, one of repentance despite his own sinlessness. Nor, on the other hand, should these temptations be weakly acceded to and their fruits embraced. The first way would be tantamount to a rejection of the world, the second a capitulation to its values. We have, like Christ, to suffer many things both for our own growth into the knowledge of love and for the sake of the world, that it be lifted up by our life's witness to the truth.

When we move in our own integrity, we can confront the many illusions conjured by the prince of this world who is also the prince of darkness. Then alone do we cease to look for external security such as is offered by worldly power. And so we can indeed withstand the temptations to corruption around us not simply with a virtuous sense of revulsion but with a larger understanding born of suffering and fructified by love. This love alone can redeem the world from the darkness of despair to the open-hearted acceptance of the light that penetrates even the most appalling circumstances. So does the crucifixion of the innocent bring to pass the resurrection of all created things to their fulfilment in God. Then we may fear no evil, for love has transformed even it to the light of God's purpose.

Acknowledgements

The author and publishers are grateful to use extracts from *Four Quartets* by T.S. Eliot, which are reprinted by permission of Faber and Faber Ltd, London.

Fount Paperbacks

Fount is one of the leading paperback publishers of religious books and below are some of its recent titles.

- [ ] THE WAY OF THE CROSS Richard Holloway £1.95
- [ ] LIKE WIND ON THE GRASSES Rita Snowden £1.95
- [ ] AN INTRODUCTION TO MARITAL
      PROBLEMS Jack Dominian £2.50
- [ ] I AM WITH YOU John Woolley £2.95
- [ ] NOW AND FOR EVER Anne Townsend £1.95
- [ ] THE PERFECTION OF LOVE Tony Castle £2.95
- [ ] A PROPHETIC PEOPLE Clifford Hill £2.95
- [ ] THOMAS MORE Richard Marius £7.95
- [ ] WALKING IN THE LIGHT David Winter £1.95
- [ ] HALF WAY Jim Thompson £2.50
- [ ] THE HEART OF THE BIBLE George Appleton £4.95
- [ ] I BELIEVE Trevor Huddleston £1.75
- [ ] PRESENT CONCERNS C. S. Lewis £1.95
- [ ] PSALMS OF PRAISE Frances Hogan £2.50
- [ ] MOTHER TERESA: CONTEMPLATIVE IN THE
      HEART OF THE WORLD Angelo Devananda £2.50
- [ ] IN THE HURRICANE Adrian Hastings £2.50

All Fount paperbacks are available at your bookshop or news-agent, or they can be ordered by post from Fount Paperbacks, Cash Sales Department, G.P.O. Box 29, Douglas, Isle of Man, British Isles. Please send purchase price plus 15p per book, maximum postage £3. Customers outside the UK send purchase price, plus 15p per book. Cheque, postal order or money order. No currency.

NAME (Block letters)_____

ADDRESS_____

_____

While every effort is made to keep prices low, it is sometimes necessary to increase them at short notice. Fount Paperbacks reserve the right to show new retail prices on covers which may differ from those previously advertised in the text or elsewhere.